101 Tips For A Beginner Internet Marketer: How To Make Your First $1,000 Online

By Christian Swift

April 2015 Edition.
Copyright © Christian Swift 2015 & Onwards.

Cover & Internal Design by Christian Swift & Joanne Moore.

All rights reserved. No part of this book may be reproduced in any form or by any electronic or mechanical means including information storage and retrieval systems – except in the case of brief quotations in articles or reviews – without the permission in writing from its publisher, Christian Swift.

All brand names and product names used in this book are trademarks, registered trademarks, or trade names of their respective holders. I am not associated with any product or vendor in this book.

ISBN-13: 978-1502477804
ISBN-10: 1502477807

Disclaimer

The strategies in this book are not to be interpreted as a guarantee or promise of earnings. Any business venture or opportunity has the possibility of significant financial risk if you don't do your own due diligence first and or get appropriate professional advice. No guarantees of specific results are expressly made or implied, and we do everything we can to ensure that we accurately represent all of the ideas, concepts, products and services and their potential of earning money for business men and women who apply them correctly.

Any examples of results (income earned or otherwise) and forward-looking statements are not necessarily typical or average, and are not intended as your proposed potential earnings. They simply express our opinion of what it is possible to achieve or earn through what we teach. Your individual results may vary widely, and we do not guarantee that your results will be similar to ours or anyone else's, or even that you will achieve any results at all. This is because your level of success in achieving results from using our products and information depends on your dedication, desire, specific applications, finances, motivation and various skills. As these factors vary from person to person, we cannot guarantee your success or income level, and we are not responsible for any of your actions.

This book is dedicated to those who follow their dreams and strive for greatness; you guys really do make the world go around.

I have included a free resources page with this book, which will give you links to all of the resources mentioned throughout the book in one easy place. Be sure to visit the link below to access it.

Here's the Link for Your Free Internet Resources Page - http://wp.me/P2twvK-b4

Also, be sure to go to the link below to grab your **free copy of our eBook** 'The 7 Horrendous Mistakes Beginner Internet Marketers Make in Their Business That Stop Them From Ever Making Any Money Online!"

Here's The Link to Claim Your Free eBook - http://wp.me/P2twvK-n6

Website

http://www.theinternetmarketingplace.com

Facebook

http://www.facebook.com/theinternetmarketingplace

Twitter

https://twitter.com/InterMarkPlace

Google+

https://plus.google.com/+TheinternetmarketingplaceGPlus

Table of Contents

Introduction 6
Creating a Website 8
Growing Your Email List 30
Producing Products That Sell 52
Marketing and Sales 74
Affiliate Marketing 104
A Few Last Pointers… 124
The Next Steps… 128
About The Author 130

Introduction

As somebody completely new to internet marketing, your success depends on getting the right information as to how to create a stable income online as fast as possible. If you could have one place where all the crucial information for beginners was all in the same place, and you could just dive in and find the answers you need to build your business, then you would get to that place of stability much faster.

'101 Tips for a Beginner Internet Marketer' is your reference library where you can find all the information that a beginner internet marketer needs to take them from a complete beginner, to having a stable income in the internet marketing business. You're about to get access to the tips and tricks that will allow you to master your understanding of the basics of online marketing – whether that is creating your own products and affiliate offers, building a website and blog to support your business, learning how to market your offers to your target audience, or a whole host of other building blocks that are crucial to your business.

So, congratulations on taking the first step towards your internet success! Many new internet marketers try franticly to put together a business and fail simply because they haven't invested their time in the right education. The foundations of their business are built on sand, and not solid rock. You on the other hand are a calculated action taker, and have made a fantastic decision in investing in yourself and your education. This book will be the resource that allows you to crack the customer code online and benefit from the passive income from an online business that you so desire. I wish you the best of luck, and I am sure that with perseverance you will make all your dreams come true.

All the best,

Christian Swift.

Chapter 1

Creating a Website

Your website is a fundamental part of your business. It is the face of your company online, and can sell while you sleep – 7 days a week!

Creating a fantastic website which can bring you in leads all year round will be a huge asset to your company, and will provide a constant stream of business. It is something tangible that somebody can point their friend to and say: 'check this company out, they make really good products'.

Bad websites on the other hand cost you money in lost business, and of course would cause huge damage to your company's reputation - so it is extremely important to get your website right.

Take action and implement these steps and you will be well on the way to turning your website into the killer lead-generation tool that it can be!

1.) Finding Your Niche/Defining Your Target Audience

One of the most daunting tasks that a beginner internet marketer faces is in finding a hot niche market to work with in the first place! Many internet marketers have a fear of building a business that they spend hours and hours over, only to discover that they were in the wrong niche in the first place! The best way to avoid that is to get your niche research right the first time around, by making sure that you are targeting a hot market who want to buy what you can offer.

"Don't lean your ladder against the wrong wall!"

When you start this search of finding a good niche, you must have somewhere to start. A perfect place for many people to start is by researching the niches that they are already knowledgeable on, to see if they contain hot niche markets that they can create and sell products in.

Is there any particular area that you are knowledgeable on that you can create products in to sell?

Who can you help, in any way? What problem do you know how to solve, that somebody would pay you to solve?

What are you passionate about?

If you are an expert in a particular niche, and that niche buys products that you can make and sell, then you are already a step ahead of all the other new internet marketers online who may have to research a particular niche in order to create products to sell – or otherwise relevant affiliate offers.

A great place to do niche research is on Google. Google AdWords has a tool called the Google Keyword planner. This tool will show you how many monthly searches a particular keyword or phrase has on Google and Google's search partners. Simply search for your niche and see how big the demand is - the more monthly searches the better! Aim to have 30,000 monthly searches for a broad topic to ensure that there is substantial interest.

That broad topic can then be narrowed down by searching particular sections of the topic to find a niche. For example, if you looked at real estate, you could break that down into lettings, how to deal with estate agents, how to go through the buying process, and many other niches. You could then search the popularity of those niches to test demand and narrow down your list even more.

Do be aware that niche markets are different to markets. Let me give you an example: Zumba is a type of dance class that is very popular at the moment – learning how to run Zumba classes is a *niche market* – whereas dancing itself is a market. Be sure to narrow down and niche your business to make sure that you aren't targeting too broad a market.

When you begin to type in a phrase on Google, it has a drop-down menu that finishes your sentences and suggests popular phrases or words. This feature is called Google Suggest. Good Suggest is great for seeing popular trends and searches (and hot niches) and it will actually suggest them to you!

Don't stop until you find a hot niche to work in that you are passionate about, and that is popular enough to create a business in.

If you need more information on finding a niche market, then it is available here - http://wp.me/p2twvK-94.

2.) Getting up and Running!

Setting up a site can seem daunting at first if you are new to internet marketing, however it doesn't have to be. Here is the process for setting up a basic site:

1. **Buy a domain name from a domain name provider**, we use www.adomainname4you.com as they are fairly cheap and have a great service. Another one to try is www.1&1.com, although sometimes they can be a bit more expensive. Domain names normally

cost around $6-8 for a .co.uk address, and around $10-12 for a .com address.

2. **Buy hosting from a hosting service.** We use www.hostgator.com for all of our web hosting and can recommend them – we have never had any problems! Other hosting companies include 1&1, 123Reg and GoDaddy.

3. **Install the type of website package that you would like to work with.** As a beginner in internet marketing, we recommend that you use a website building package to build your website, instead of getting into coding it all yourself (or paying someone else to do it!). We normally use WordPress for all of our sites as it is simple to use once installed, and has lots of high quality plug-ins which are fantastic for everything from building website pages, to optimizing your website. WordPress is free to use; you will need to download it, and then install it onto your domain name (do this inside your webhosting account – eg. Hostgator.com).

You can find all of these websites and resources, and all the other websites mentioned in this book on your *resources page* (the link that you need to visit is contained within the opening pages of this book).

3.) Make Sure You That Have a Blog and Update it on a Regular Basis

There are so many internet marketers who do not give away regular, free, value-packed content, and then wonder why customers do not buy their products! Customers like to sample your work, and a blog is a great way to engage with your customers, present and future, and get them to like you and what you have to offer.

Blogs should be updated at least 1-2 times per week with fresh content, as if you go quiet, customers will think that you have run out of information to give them!

If you are using WordPress, then creating articles for your blog is very simple. Look on your Dashboard for where it says 'add post', click that, and then all you have to do is write the article and click 'publish'. You can also add a plug-in that allows you to fill out SEO information to help rank your website better in search engines, there are plenty available if you search in the 'plugins' section of WordPress.

4.) Give Three Things in Your Blogs…

There are three main things that you need to include in your blog posts to make them resonate with your audience in the best way possible. Here they are in no particular order:

- **Give GREAT content.** It goes without saying that people will only come back to your blog if they liked the content that you gave them the first time they visited. Make sure that you update your blog and give some great free content to get people to come back!

- **Reveal some personal information about yourself.** Once in a while it is a great idea to write a blog post that is a lot more personal and that reveals some information about yourself – for example, if you did a blog post on your 10 greatest fears as a start-up business owner. Revealing personal information allows the reader to get that much closer to you, so that they feel like they really know you and have connected with you. That way, they will be enticed to come back to your blog and see your next update!

- **Include some controversial content.** This is a great way to open up a discussion on your blog posts. If you include controversial content then it is more likely to be shared online, which will attract more people to your blog.

Include these three things on a consistent basis, and you will be onto a winner!

5.) Create a Squeeze-Page to Capture Visitors' Details and Get Them onto Your Email List

You <u>must</u> have a squeeze-page form on every page of your website (excluding *Membership Pages, 'legal' pages, your contact page, or pages where you are selling a product or service*) to sign visitors up to your emails/newsletter. This can be done by using a 'widget' (we will guide you through how to do this later on!), which can then by put onto the side bar of your website on every page.

Your end goal is to get your visitors onto your email list. From there you can give them more free information, and eventually sell to them too. Always remember: **The money is in the list!**

You can also create website pages called 'landing pages', which are where people who land on the page fill in their details to get onto your list in return for a freebie. The freebie is commonly a free report, free online course or free video series; but it can be anything at all that adds value.

We use a fantastic tool for creating our landing-pages called OptimizePress. It is a plug-in for WordPress, and it makes creating website pages a piece of cake! Joanne and I wrote an article about it especially for you, you can check it out here - http://tinyurl.com/opwg2al.

6.) Don't Call The Homepage to Your Website 'Welcome to Our Website!'

A big mistake that a lot of beginner internet marketers make is putting 'welcome to our website' at the top of the homepage on their website. This is a **big** mistake and will have people clicking off your website faster than you could imagine!

The homepage on your website is prime real-estate, and is best used for giving away a free eBook or online course to get the visitor to sign up to your email list - or to capture their interest by making a big, bold promise of telling them how you can help them. That way, you will have more potential customers to market to on your email list, and you will convert more of your website visitors into paying customers long-term.

When somebody visits your website for the first time, they are interested in what you can offer them. So make sure to get your freebies and free articles in front of them right away to keep them engaged!

7.) Focus The Website Around Your Customer, Not Around Your Company

Have you ever heard the expression *'it's the sizzle that sells the sausage'*?

Customers are interested in what your products can DO for them, and are not in the least interested in how long your company have been in operation or your credentials… at least to begin with.

If you are going to put information about your story on your website, then create an 'about us' page on the navigation bar so they can see it if they want it!

There are **two** types of website visitors: those who come across your website because they have a specific problem that needs fixing, and those that stumble across your website because they are just flicking around the internet. Your website needs to cater for both of these types and must be focused on **adding massive value** to your customer initially to help them get over a problem, or capture their interest.

Don't spend lots of time talking about your story, your company or when you got into business. They don't know you from Adam at this point and will not care. Give away freebies, write informative blog posts and add value to the customer *right off the bat* to get their attention, get their details and get them into your sales funnel!

8.) Make Sure That You Create Your Website with Functionality in Mind. Make it Easy to Navigate for the User for Higher Engagement

Focus on making your website easily navigable for the user. Make sure that you have a navigation bar that stays at the top of your website to help the visitor easily find what they want.

Sometimes website owners with blogs try and use confusing category names for their blog posts, and sometimes even for the navigation bar on their website! Use simple, easy to understand categories on your website to ensure that your visitors get the best experience possible.

Users who arrive from another website will need to see right away what your website has to offer for them, and must be able to navigate around the site easily. The bar at the top of your webpages will most likely be the place they start. Keep the layouts on every page easy to read and easy to understand, remember K.I.S.S – Keep It Simple Stupid!

9.) Make Sure That You Have a 'Contact us' Page, and Have a Way to Contact You on Every Page

If people want to contact you to offer you business, then they shouldn't have to flick around your whole website just to find your contact details. It is good practice to have your contact details in the footer of every webpage, or as a widget on the side of the page so that they are easily accessible, and make it as easy as possible for people to contact you!

You should also create a 'contact us' page in your navigation bar at the top. You can get them to submit a question online on that page, they can then ask their question and leave their email address. That way they do not have to actually open up their email inbox and manually insert your email address to contact you. The little things make your site better for the customer!

10.) Make Your Website Individual

Never try to copy another company's website! If people are searching for information online, or looking for a website to buy an information product from, they will be more likely to disregard websites which are all the same and go for the one which is unique. This is sometimes because they think that the others must all be affiliate websites trying to sell them the same thing!

A lot of internet marketers fall down by advertising in a 'me too' sort of way on their site. You need to make your website individual for you to stand out and make people remember you.

Even if you are working as an affiliate, you could create a page to give your opinion on the affiliate product that you are offering, to make it more personal. Think of it as providing a personal testimonial for the viewer that the product is worth investing in. Never let your business solely rely around somebody else if you are an affiliate. Make it personal!

11.) Look at Your Site Through The Eyes of Your Customer… Look for Information and Shop on Your Own Site!

Here's a fun test: imagine you are a customer and have a look around your website… How does it look? Does it feel professional? Does it feel relaxed and welcoming? Are there any free bits that you can sample? Is it easy to find the information or products that you need?

Looking around your site in the eyes of a customer is one of the most productive things that you can do! Sometimes it is best to take a step back from *creating* to just think about how you can better what you already have.

You could even go a step further and ask somebody to be a 'mystery shopper' for your site. Ask them to give you honest feedback based on how they rate the site in terms of functionality, content and how professional it appears; and then be sure to make the changes necessary to improve your site.

12.) Gather Plenty of Testimonials For Your Website and For Your Services... Try to Get People on the 'Inside'

Gathering positive testimonials for your site and your products/services is one of the most positive things you can do for your site, as they act as social proof for both you and your business. They tell your potential customers that the fears that they have around signing up for you freebies, your blog, your mailing list or buying your products/services are simply not true.

Be sure to include the full name of the testimonial giver, and be sure to have testimonials on EVERY page where you sell a product. If you haven't sold any products and have no testimonials then give away a freebie or do a service for free to get some testimonials. The more the merrier!

Another strategy to use on your site is to show people how amazing it is 'on the inside', i.e. When they have signed up to your newsletter or bought your products. Testimonials are an amazing way to do this. Make sure to make the grass look greener on the other side to stop them just following your blog and not signing up to your list/buying your products! It is the sense of community that will lure them in with this strategy.

13.) Make Sure That Everything on Your Site is Relevant

One of the biggest turnoffs for a potential customer is to land on your website and be faced with lots of pointless images, or to see a lot of irrelevant information that doesn't help them in any way. Pointless images or text will just aid as distractions, and will most likely end in your potential customer clicking off your site. You need to fulfil their immediate need – strong, free direction and information leading to a sale later down the line.

We strongly advise that you only post content on your site that your customers will LOVE and that will give them value or let them know about your services.

This brings me onto…

14.) Don't Hide Your Products Away!

When beginner internet marketers start to advertise they go one of two ways…

1- They plaster their products all over every page of their website (or online in places like forums) and hope that people will buy them without offering any free value first.

2- Or they offer plenty of free value, but do not even have links to their main products on the navigation bar on the front of the website – or anywhere else for that matter!

It is all about getting the balance right. Make sure that you add LOTS of value on your website before you expect people to buy from you. But at the same time, new visitors to the site need to know what your company is about and what products you sell.

For that reason it is a good idea to have a section on the navigation bar at the top of your website that new visitors can click onto and see what products or services that you/your company offer. You will not get a lot of sales from this area of the website; but you are putting it plainly to the customer that you are there to sell your knowledge to them and help them!

15.) Personalise Your Site for Higher Engagement

People like to buy from people that they know, like and trust; so it is important to always appear personable to your potential customers and fans.

A great way to increase the engagement that you get from viewers is to personalise your website, and put images of yourself on there. That way, potential customers can see who they are buying from, and this will increase the trust that they have with you (and it will also increase your sales figures!).

It is also a good idea to do a blog post every once in a while that contains more personal information – for example, the challenges that you faced when you started in your business, or the fears that you had. This will increase engagement as people will be able to empathise with what you are writing.

Videos are also a great way to increase engagement, and they are shown to increase engagement by 300% on average! Take advantage of the use of video to turn viewers into raving fans.

16.) Get The Legals of Your Website Sorted – Boring But Necessary!

There are an assortment of legal measures and disclaimers that you will need to get up on your website in order to sell nationally or internationally (for your own business). You are likely to need:

- An Anti-Spam Policy

- A Full Set Of Terms & Conditions

- Legal Contact Information (With your trading address)

- An Earnings Disclaimer (depending on what you are selling)

- A Privacy Policy

What you need on your website will vary depending on whether you are selling your own products, or whether you are acting as an affiliate.

Be sure to get proper legal advice on this, as the rules change depending on which country you are selling from. But as a rule you will always need a privacy policy and a full set of Terms and Conditions, but again these will be country specific.

17.) Optimize Your Site for Mobile Users

Too many internet marketers have websites that work fine on a desktop or laptop computer, but aren't optimized for mobile users.

Many people flick around on the internet on their mobiles looking for answers and information to help them while they are outside in public on the train, in the park or even in bed! You need to make sure that your website can cater for these users too; otherwise you may be throwing away a lot of potential business!

And by the way, whether your site is mobile-responsive is now also a ranking factor in the Google algorithm – meaning that you will be penalised if yours isn't!

The plug-in for WordPress that we use to build our webpages automatically formats them for mobile users as well as computer users. Check out the article we wrote especially for you on OptimizePress here - http://tinyurl.com/opwg2al!

18.) The Use of Widgets on Your Website

Have you ever been onto a website that has adverts or testimonials that run down the side of the page? These are called widgets (on a WordPress site), and you can install them on your own website page, so that you can advertise, put testimonials up, or put up many other visual aids for your viewers to see!

Widgets can be set to only appear on a particular website page that you set them to, or you can set them to appear on every page on a part of your website - for example on your blog - if you wanted testimonials running down the side of the page.

If you don't have a WordPress site, then you will need somebody experienced in coding to help you create the widgets, and help put them onto your website on selected pages.

If you wish to come up with the design of the widget yourself, then you will probably need to send the coder the picture that you would like to use.

Once you have the coding, then, copy and paste the coding into the 'text' widget to create your custom widget. We recommend finding a coder on sites such as Elance.com or Upwork.com if you wish to go down that route.

However, if you do have WordPress installed on your site, then you can access the widget menu by going onto 'appearance' on the side panel, and then selecting the widget that you want to use. You can then fill out the details from there.

19.) Optimise Your Site for Loading Speed

It is a hard fact to face that if your site takes more than 5 seconds to load, then most web-users who have come across your website will just click the back button on their web-browsers – and you will most likely lose them forever.

To stop his from happening, make sure that you optimize your website for loading speed, as well as customer engagement. A simple way to speed up your website is to make sure to empty the website cache regularly (there are plenty of WordPress plugins that do this – just search in the plugins area).

A big drain on website loading speed is the media that you put on your webpages. Instead of uploading .jpg picture files, try and upload pictures as .png files as these take less time to load. Try and also remove irrelevant pictures and media to speed up loading time.

There is also the option of paying for faster hosting if your website really is slowing down loading speed!

20.) Make Sure That Your Update Services are Set Correctly

If you have a WordPress blog, then it is a great idea to make sure that your blog is updating online 'bookmarking' services correctly. These bookmarking services are pinged by your blog every time you make a new blog post, and they help spread the word about your website so that your pages can get indexed by Google quicker.

To view the update services on a WordPress site go to 'Settings' on the side-panel of your blog, and then 'Writing', and then scroll down to where it has a list of web URLs (the first one is always http://rpc.pingomatic.com).

The trick is to make sure that all your bookmarking sites on there are up-to-date. You can search for a list on Google for the best bookmarking sites in the current year. This will help make sure that your website blogs get listed quicker, and that traffic builds up organically to your site.

21.) Configure Your Sidebars for Maximum Engagement

Here's a great, quick tip – configure your sidebars for maximum engagement. It is proven that on a website, sidebars on the right side of the webpage get more engagement than sidebars on the left side of a webpage (especially adverts and information on the top right-hand side of the right sidebar).

Be sure to put all the most important parts of your toolbars on the top-right side of your webpages - such as your opt-in box for your email list - and put all the other less important parts of the sidebar below that.

Little tweaks like these that increase profits can take years of testing to find, and a lot of money. My aim is to pass on as many as possible to you throughout this book to save you time and money.

Chapter 2

Growing Your Email List

To survive in any business - no matter whether online or offline - you need to get good at both getting leads for your business, and converting those leads into paying customers. The art of capturing leads is fairly simple when you have the knowledge and understanding. It is converting those leads into paying customers which is the part that proves hard for many businesses.

In this chapter, I am going to teach you the basics of gathering leads – potential customers to put through your sales funnel. I am also going to give you some tips and advice that took Joanne (my business partner) and I years of practice to discover, which will increase your conversions from those leads substantially if learned and applied!

Let's get into it.

22.) Get an Auto-Responder

Before you get started with capturing leads for your business, you will need to set up the necessary systems to manage correspondence with your email list.

Firstly, you will need an auto-responder to send out email broadcasts to your list on your behalf. Auto-responders are brilliant systems which allow you to write emails and set them to send out at any particular time of day, any day of the week!

There are plenty of fantastic auto-responders out there, ranging from auto-responders with free trails, to auto-responders which are paid-for only from the start. To name a few commonly used ones there are: GetResponse, MailChimp, AWeber and Infusionsoft.

MailChimp is free to send out email broadcasts (emails that you have written, but that have to be sent out now. You can't set them to send out at a certain time, like in an auto-responder sequence), however you will have to pay for the auto-responder system. It is good for getting started and sending out basic emails, and it is really easy to navigate.

GetResponse is currently only $12 monthly for 1,000 subscribers (which is very cheap!). It also has fantastic functionality, and I can highly recommend it, as we use it for many of our projects.

AWeber has a great $1 trial that you can start using while you are learning that is also a great deal. However, it is slightly more expensive than GetResponse after you come out of the free trial.

The Infusionsoft auto-responder is a lot more expensive as it comes in a package with other products for over

$150 per month, it is also a lot more technical. We do not recommend it for beginners, but if you have a bit of experience with Auto-Responders already, then it is easy to learn.

To get you started, we recommend either using GetResponse, MailChimp or starting with the $1 trail with AWeber - it really is all personal preference as they all offer a great service.

You can find links to all these Auto-Responders on your *resources page* (you can find the link at the front of this book).

23.) You Now Need a Customer Relationship Management System (CRM system)

A Customer Relationship Management system (CRM system for short) is a MUST for your business, in order to keep track of everybody who has signed up to your list: their details, their preferences, what day and time they signed up and much more!

Sometimes a CRM system will come built-into your auto-responder, but with others, you may have to get an external CRM system to interlink with your auto-responder to get them to talk to each other and share information.

Don't worry, it's not as technical as it sounds at first!

If you go into the settings area in your auto-responder system, there will be a list of CRM systems which link to your chosen auto-responder. It is just a case of following the instructions and then all of the rest is done for you!

As well as GetResponse, we use Infusionsoft, and in Infusionsoft our auto-responder system and CRM system are one and the same as they are all in one program. It sure is handy to have all the details in one place!

However, if you are going with another auto-responder except Infusionsoft, then Capsule CRM and Zoho CRM are two great CRM systems that partner with most Auto-Responders (you can find links to these on the *resources page*).

If you live in the UK, you will need to register your company for data protection with the ICO to be allowed to store and use sensitive data. This is a fairly simple process and costs £35 a year to be covered. If you live abroad, then please check the rules on holding personal data where you live.

Keeping data on your list up to date is a fantastic way to stay tuned to their preferences and communicate with them in the right way.

For example, if somebody opted into your list by receiving one particular freebie, then you can tag them as having received that freebie, so that you do not offer it to them again. This makes it easy to build lists of people who have bought particular products or services, so that you can market something else to them – without having to keep a physical list of all that information! Clever right?

24.) The Money is in The List!

An email list is by far one of the biggest, if not **the** biggest asset that an internet-based business can have. Having a great list really is like having a licence to print money! A list of customers is FAR more valuable than a list of prospects, and on average a list of people who have bought from you previously are up to **15 times** more likely to buy from you again.

Always focus on building your list, as your list is what is going to give you long-term stability in your business.

It gives you a warm feeling inside when you know that you have a responsive list that you can launch a product to on demand. Especially when you know that that product will produce a lot of sales, and will genuinely help your customers.

Your list is something constant that nobody can take away from you. People can copy your content, your sales funnels or the way that you write your emails – but they can never get hold of your list!

25.) Give Away (Free) Value!

Getting leads into your sales funnel is simple... give something away for free! This could either be a free report, a free eBook, or even a free course – that's up to you. What's for sure is that giving a freebie away is a great way to give away some of your work/education to somebody so that they can sample your teachings in return for their contact details.

Why do you need their contact details? Because that way, you can sell to them again and again using your auto-responder, CRM system, direct mail and phone calls!

You will need to create a page on your website advertising your freebie which has boxes for them to sign up (by filling in their details) to receive it. OptimizePress and LeadPages are two great tools for effortlessly building squeeze pages. We use OptimizePress, but LeadPages is great too (if not a bit expensive).

The standard details to ask for in return for the freebie are the name and email of the customer.

Some marketers only ask for an email address, as this can cause a higher conversion rate on the page (the amount of people who opt-in to get the freebie vs. the total views of the page). We have personally found that leads we obtain through asking for their name AND email end up staying in our sales funnel longer and buying more products, so we strongly recommend asking for both the name AND the email.

26.) Write as if you are Speaking to a Single Person

Writing your emails and sales copy as if you are speaking to a single person is **hugely** important! Your readers want to feel like you are sending them a **personal email**, so talking as if you are addressing them alone is a must.

Writing in this fashion is very powerful, and it will hugely increase the engagement that you will get from your readers. People buy from people that they like and trust, so it is important to be personal and selective with your emails.

It will massively increase your bottom-line after all!

27.) Single or Double Opt-in?

A really big debate (which is always in the spotlight on internet marketing forums!) is whether to use what is known as a single or a double opt-in when somebody enters their contact details into your squeeze page.

A single opt-in is when a contact only has to input their contact details once before they receive your freebie and officially 'join your list'. Whereas with a double opt-in, the contact has to input their details and then confirm their opt-in by clicking on a confirmation link in an automatically generated email that they receive after initially opting in.

There are merits to using either of these approaches. A double opt-in list is normally more responsive when emailed as they have double opted-in very purposefully, and are really excited to be in your list. A single opt-in list can be less responsive, as during any marketing campaign there will always be the 'freebie chasers' as we call them who just sign up to any list to get a freebie!

Although that said, there is an argument that if you are using double opt-ins then you are leaving a lot of money on the table. Our research shows that single opt-in lists may be bigger and less responsive, but they can be built quicker than double opt-in lists, and still yield brilliant sales. Leads can be lost when asking visitors to double opt-in, so there will be fewer people in your list to help and sell to.

We personally use single opt-in lists as we do a lot of solo ads (covered later in the book), and we would leave a lot of money on the table by asking people to opt-in twice. However, it is a personal decision for you and your business and there is no right answer!

28.) Build a Relationship

In simple terms, talking to your list is about building a relationship with leads (potential customers) so that they end up becoming raving fans and buying your products!

Giving away a freebie is the first step in that relationship, and in a way the most important. First impressions definitely count when trying to gain credibility with your leads, a good first impression will make them want to come back for more.

Make sure that you keep in mind when you are communicating with your list that you are constantly trying to build a relationship, and add value for free at the same time as trying to sell your products/services. Always give them at least three emails where you give them rock-solid information that will help them before you ask for the first sale!

29.) Nurture vs. Straight-Sell

From the moment that you capture a lead, you have a decision to make about how you are going to work with it. That decision is the nurture vs. straight-sell balance.

A couple of years ago, the approach was to give away a freebie to capture a lead's details, and then to nurture that lead for several weeks by sending out free (and valuable) information. This was simply to get them to like you and what you teach, and to gain trust.

You would then offer them your products/services further down the line when you have a solid long-term *relationship* with that lead so that they trust your paid-for information to be worthy of their spend.

However these days, people receive more and more emails than ever before. They might be incredibly busy and may just scan through your email, not paying it much attention. This is when the new theory came into practice: the *straight-sell*.

Straight-selling is doing exactly what it says on the tin - selling to your customer straight away, right from the get-go. And I mean right from the get-go.

The best place to sell to your lead as soon as you receive it, is on the thank-you page where they download their freebie. That is the last time you will speak to 100% of your leads before some opt-out, or never read your emails again.

Now don't get me wrong, I'm not telling you to send email after email selling to your leads. You still need to send out emails giving them value so that they are interested in your information. But the theory says that it is better to give them the opportunity of a buying a product/service *straight away*, so that they don't just receive your free emails and then never buy from you.

We do a mixture of nurturing and straight-selling in our business as we sell to our customers straight-off-the-bat, but we also send out valuable information on our emails so that we don't just get a wave of unsubscribers. It is about finding the correct balance between adding value to get your customer interested, and selling your products and/or services.

30.) Survey Your Email List

One fantastic tip that will massively help in converting your list into paying clients is to make sure that you survey your list on a regular basis – and learn from the results.

Surveys are a very powerful tool as if you send out a survey to your list, then they will feel like you care and genuinely want to help them (and not just sell to them). However, that is not the only benefit… surveys also give you an incredible insight into the needs and wants of your potential customer.

Say if you were in the Internet Marketing niche, and asked your list a question like: 'what are your most pressing questions that you need answering about internet marketing?', then by the responses you will know the questions your target audience are asking. Enabling you to create the products that give them the answers! Make sure that you survey your email list at least once every couple of months to keep up with their needs and the 'hot' topics in your niche.

There are some great survey tools out there that aren't too expensive: Survey Monkey is a fantastic tool, but requires a small financial investment (we would recommend it!). Kwik Survey is a free and unlimited service and another one to check out – have a look at your *resources page* for the relevant links.

31.) Use Attraction-Based Marketing

Another tip for communicating effectively with your list is to use attraction-based marketing.

Normally when you market your products and services to potential clients you make all the effort to draw them in to a webpage to buy your offer, and you may use special discounts, added bonuses and other means to 'go to' your customer. The difference with attraction marketing is that the roles are reversed and you get your customer to come to you!

Let me give you an example of attraction marketing in practice: let's say that there is somebody called John on your list; you could send out a message to John and simply say 'Hello John, Could you please call me on 07*** ****** to discuss helping you with your marketing, many thanks, Christian'.

You can send these messages out in bulk to your list using your auto-responder, yet they seem very personal to receive. There is a function in every auto-responder where you can set the email you are writing to address each individual recipient by their first name (that is saved in your CRM system).

These messages will give your communication a personal touch and will rocket-boost sales conversions from your list. Everybody likes to be given special treatment!

32.) Frequency

There is a common saying in the Internet Marketing world, which is: 'Contact your leads until they buy, die or go away!'. However, this doesn't mean that you should spam your leads with constant emails and sales tactics; it simply means that you should be contacting your leads on a frequent basis, literally until they buy, die or unsubscribe!

So what does 'on a frequent basis' actually mean in terms of how often? Well we contact our list 2-3 times a week, and the emails that we send out are a mixture of free content/blog post reminders (to build the relationship), and sales emails. We generally sell once to twice a week.

Many internet marketers think that selling through email twice a week is too much. But remember that of every batch of emails that you send out, some will be deleted straight away, some may never be seen; and of the ones that are seen they may only be skim-read through quickly. You need to ensure that you are sending out enough emails to firstly get them read, and also to email often enough to provide enough sales for your business.

Also, please do remember that sales emails are not generally a pitch in an email; they are generally designed to move people onto a sales page which has an offer – you are not actually selling in a sales email!

33.) Use Multiple Offers

If customers are not buying from your sales emails (and therefore sales pages) over a sustained period of time, then either you do not have a good enough relationship with your list, or there is something wrong with the offer itself.

In the case of the latter, try changing the offer in some way to try and entice them to buy… This could be by a number of ways - either by lowering the price of the offer, chucking in added freebies, trying to sell to them over the phone (if you have their number) instead of email, or by a whole host of other options.

If they never end up buying the product, then change the offer totally and try and sell them something else! The key to develop the relationship (before leading to the sale) is to keep in frequent contact with your list, making sure that you are adding *massive value* as much as you can.

34.) Don't Neglect Going Postal!

Some people in this world are simply old fashioned and love holding physical sales copy! Make sure that you don't forget these people – be sure to send out physical sales copy in the post every now and then so that you can expand your offer to a wider market.

If you do not send out physical sales copy to these recipients, then they are not very likely to ever buy from you - assuming they don't buy online. Plus, it's more personal and will have a bigger impact and leave a bigger impression than an email, as not a lot of online companies use direct mail anymore.

35.) Offer Your Customers a Direct Experience of You

The two highest converting sales tactics in any business are:

1- Selling one-to-one in a private consultation

2- Selling on stage to a small, select group of people

Therefore, a fantastic way to convert your list into paying customers is to invite them to get a direct experience of you and your company. This can either be through events in person - such as private free consultations – or by inviting your 'tribe' to an afternoon or evening event for free so that you can teach them and upsell them to your products/services.

It could even be through a teleseminar (where you get lots of people on the phone at the same time, teach them some great content, and then sell at the end), or a webinar (an online seminar).

Giving your potential customers a personal experience of you and your business will leave more of a lasting impression, and will result in higher sales conversions!

36.) Prioritise Your List, and They Will Prioritise You Too!

Your list is made up of your best customers, those who have bought from you on multiple occasions, follow your brand and will likely buy from you again many times in the future.

If you treat these customers with priority, then they will prioritise you in the future when they look to buy products and/or services that you can offer them, when they have the need.

There are many ways in which you can prioritise customers on your list. For example if you are going to run a live event, then you could send the customers on your list 'VIP' tickets which are specially reserved for them, and are at a lower price than the other tickets available normally.

You could also invite the customers on your list to your event before the main public, so that they have the opportunity to buy tickets before anybody else (priority tickets).

These are just a few examples of how you can prioritise the customers on your list to build greater rapport with them. Besides, prioritising customers who have bought from you before normally results in more sales, as it is a lot easier to sell to somebody who has bought from you before than it is to acquire a totally new customer.

So, learn to prioritise those on your list and build a lasting relationship – what you give you will receive!

37.) Guest Blogging to Grow Your List

One great way that you can grow your email list of prospects is by doing guest blogs on other blog sites in your niche, and then having a 'call to action' at the end of your post to give away a freebie and get the viewer to sign up to your email list.

Many blog owners will allow you to do a 'guest blog' on their site as long as your content is of a good quality. It makes their job easier as a blogger as they won't have to write content for their website for that day; and as they allow you to promote your own link, service or product at the bottom of the post in return, it doesn't directly cost them any money.

So make sure that you get contacting a few other blog owners in your niche to ask them if you could do a guest blog in return for a link to your site (where visitors can sign up to your email list).

As long as you have a strong call to action then this can be a fantastic way to grow your email list – especially if they have a lot of viewers on their blog!

38.) Be Very Careful with Bought Lists – if You Use Them at all!

Here is one tip that will save you money – be VERY careful with bought lists of contacts. Some internet marketers and other list owners will allow you to buy a list of contacts, say 100,000 records of names and email addresses, for a fixed price. Be VERY careful with these lists – and here is why…

As you know, list building is all about *building a relationship* with those who you reach through your emails; and that relationship is what is going to lead them to buy your products and/or services in the future - as they will *know, like and trust you.*

If you buy an email list then you have no way of knowing how that list has been emailed before, if the contacts on the list are qualified in any way for what you offer, or if they are just a random list of names with no long-term value to you at all!

Also when you buy a list, you will have to start your own personal relationship with that list from scratch. It can be very helpful for the original list owner to contact the list and introduce you, so that the list know who you are, and why you will be emailing them. Otherwise you could have A LOT of the contacts opt-out very quickly!

Our advice is to only buy lists from those who you trust, and to try to buy highly targeted lists of contacts that are pre-qualified for your niche by the owner. An introduction also helps as aforementioned - this can be done via email or by sending them a video!

39.) Joint-Venture (JV) List Launches and Introductions

JV list launches/introductions will boost the size of your list massively... and therefore the size of your profits!

These launches involve another well-established list owner advertising your product, freebie or service to their list (for a profit split on the sales, or for you to do the same for them with your list). Or in some cases, just sending an email out to their list to let them know about your website.

For beginner internet marketers, this list sharing JV can be a HUGE breakthrough, and a great boost to their business – just think about the potential reach of your products if you had 3-5 list owners helping you promote them by emailing their lists? The potential customers reached would be trebled, if not quadrupled or *more*!

However, the real bonus is not really in the initial sales, but in the life-time value of the customers and prospects that you obtain from the launch.

Let me explain... when the JV partner directs the traffic to your site to see the product, give away your freebie, or just so that they can be introduced to your website, you can capture their details so that you can add them to your own list. This means that you can build a relationship with them, and email them again and again about your products and/or services; and the great thing is that they will be pre-qualified for your niche, as they have come from another marketer's list in your very niche!

And that is why JV launches are so powerful, because you can massively amplify your marketing reach.

Chapter 3

Producing Products That Sell

Your products are the cornerstone of your business; it is extremely important that you get them right, and that you give great good content, as they are the actual meat of your online business.

Many Internet Marketers fling together the plans for their products and create them in a desperate rush to get them online - without actually doing the correct research to check that there is a need for what they are providing.

In this chapter, the tips and knowledge gained will allow you to research what the market actually *wants at the moment*, and we will put you on the correct path to creating the best online products to sell to your chosen market to fulfil their wants and needs.

Read closely because this is where things get *really* interesting!

40.) Check What is Selling Well in Your Niche

Let's start with talking about your product strategy. Before you make a product, it is best to do some simple due diligence to make sure that there will be a demand for what you are going to create – as you want as many sales as possible right?

There are many places that you can check for what is selling well in your niche. One fantastic place is on niche-related forums. For example, if you are in the internet marketing niche, a good place to check is the WSO section of the Warrior Forum.

The Warrior Forum is the biggest internet marketing forum online, and the WSO section is the part of the website where people sell their product offers to members of the forum. These sorts of places are great for seeing what is selling well at the moment, and what is up and coming in your niche.

Another good place to check are affiliate sites such as Clickbank.com. These sites have a range of products that are selling in different categories, so you can pick the one which best fits your niche. You can then see the top selling products in your niche from there.

Another place to check is Google! Type in your niche to see the top related products, sign up to their emails and marketing campaigns, buy their products, learn from them and then make your own versions with your own spin on the subject matter.

If you pick a topic that is selling well in your chosen niche, then you have taken the first step to producing a product that will become popular, and will draw you in passive income, month on month!

41.) What Type of Expert are You?

There are *three* types of experts who produce products: **results experts**, **reporter experts** and **role model experts**. For you to create products effectively, you need to think about which type of expert you are, and create products to suit that fashion.

Results experts use their results to sell their products. They market them by commenting on their own successes with that system/product, for example 'I made $1,000,000 with this system, and you can too!'. This is a fantastic way of being an expert if you have results, but if you don't have results yet then you will have to be a reporter, or a role model expert.

Reporter experts reduce research time for their customers by learning from other experts, and compiling knowledge and information into one product or package for their customer. A beginner in any niche can still be a reporter expert by learning about the niche and creating useful products to educate their customers. To be this type of expert you just have to always remain one step ahead of your customer in terms of knowledge!

The last type of expert is the role model expert. People worldwide look up to role models to show them the way and educate them. A big example of a role model expert is the Dalai Lama. Those in his niche follow his lead for him to show them the next step.

Work out what type of expert you are in your niche, and remember what your customers expect from you as that type of expert. Whether that be knowledge, or inspiration, or both!

42.) Types of Products

There are an assortment of products that you as a creator can put together to get your message out there and give your customers value, knowledge and/or inspiration. Anybody, in any niche, can decide to do any/all of the products listed below. Decide which you would like to do, and in which order. Take some action and get started!

- ✓ eBooks
- ✓ Physical Books & Guides
- ✓ Amazon Kindle Books

- ✓ An Interview Series
- ✓ Online Courses
- ✓ Webinars
- ✓ Seminars/Live events
- ✓ Teleseminars
- ✓ Speaking Events
- ✓ Audio Courses
- ✓ DVD Programmes
- ✓ Subscription Systems/Products
- ✓ Software Tools/Programmes
- ✓ Coaching/Consulting
- ✓ Membership Sites
- ✓ Mastermind Programmes

There is no right or wrong place to start here, and everybody will have their own preference. Some will choose to start with the easiest products, while others will start with the hardest!

We recommend that you stick on your path to completion when you have chosen the product you would like to do, as jumping around creating several products at once can be troublesome and tiring.

Also, it is important to bear in mind that you will need to 'stage' your products into some sort of sales funnel or *'product staircase'*.

A product staircase is the order in which your products are presented to the potential client. For example, they might get a freebie first, and then get upsold to an eBook for $5, and then an online course for $97, and then a coaching programme for $997, and so on.

Be sure to do some planning around your product funnel so that you know exactly what route a potential customer will take through your array of products (the *hierarchy*), and what your marketing methods may be for each product.

Create a plan, stick to your guns and get it done!

43.) Remember that Most People are Beginners!

Before you start planning your product, it is important to get more of a hold on the type of individuals that you are going to be targeting with your product.

Remember that in ANY niche, there are FAR more beginners than there are experts. And for that reason, there will always be a bigger market for products aimed at beginners than products aimed at intermediates/experts.

This is no reason to ALWAYS target the beginner niche alone (unless you want to!), but remember to consider the level of expertise that you are aiming your product at in your target market for best results.

44.) Brainstorm Your Master-plan!

THE most important phase of ANY product is always the initial planning phase. This planning sets the tone for your whole product, as your plans are your basic blueprint to guide you through the creation of your product. A lot of the time when we hear about internet marketers having trouble turning their product idea into a reality, it is normally because they get lost on the journey to a finished product without their guide – *the plan*!

So to get started, find a quiet place where you are not going to be disturbed, whether that is a quiet corner in your home, or out in a public place like a café. You can either mind-map using paper, or there are some software tools which you can buy so that you can do your mind-mapping on a laptop. One example is iMindMap by Tony Buzan - check it out on your *resources page*.

Start with the basics and work upwards from there until you have the main points of your product mapped out.

First think about the main sections in your product - for example if you were making a product on how to sew, you might have a section on sewing technique, then another on the different equipment available (such as which threads or needles to use), and then a third with different sewing patterns to try.

From here you can break down these titles into sub-sections. For example, in sewing technique you could have beginner, intermediate and advanced levels. You would then break that down to decide what each of those sub-sections entail – the specifics.

Keep planning until you have each section, sub-section and all your ideas mapped out so that all you have to do is join up the dots and fill in the content. It would be a lot easier to create content if all you had to do was join up the dots of the structure right?

45.) How to Get Paid to Create a Product

If you want to start creating a product right away, or are new to creating products altogether, then here is a simple way to create your first product, and ensure that it will be a certain hit with your market. Even if you don't have a list to sell to!

It is very easy to build a small following with social media these days, so it is very easy to get a loud voice online without too much effort.

Aim to build up a small following, and then invite them to join you on a tele-seminar or webinar series that will contain content that they will *love*. Aim to get 30 on the webinar, but it doesn't matter if you fall slightly short. You can charge for each entrant; typical charges can be between £50 and £3,000 depending on your particular niche and the customer.

The teleseminar (or webinar) series can be comprised of one seminar per week, run across an 8-week period. These seminars will be recorded (many teleseminar or webinar services will do this automatically), and can then be compiled into a product that you can package up and sell to future clients.

The key here is to use surveys before and after each teleclass. These surveys are designed to extract the language of your market (which is key!), and to make sure that your product is 100% fine-tuned to your market's needs.

Before each class, you can send a survey out to those registered asking their top two questions that they would like answered around the particular subject associated with your seminar. These can then be answered on the seminar, and your clients will love your content as they got all the answers that they were looking for - and more!

After the class, you can then send out a survey to ask if there were any unanswered questions that they would like to have answered in the next class.

This means that you can 'dip your toe in the water' and actually GET PAID to create and test a product. And you can even use the language of your customers in your marketing. Double win!

46.) Feed Your Buyers by Answering Their Questions

One of THE best things you can do when creating a product is to find out what questions your prospective buyers are asking, and then answer them in your product.

There are many places which you can find out what unanswered questions your clients have, but one of the best places is on niche-related forums.

For example, if you were selling products to the Internet Marketing industry, the Warrior Forum would be a great place to start to look for questions that you can answer. Simply search through the (fairly recent) thread topics and see what the most common questions are – get these answered well, and you have a killer product already!

Another fantastic place to look is on Google AdWords. AdWords has a tool called the Google Keyword planner, and this tool shows the number of searches a month that a particular phrase or word has on Google and Google's related search networks. Simply type in the questions that you think your target market may be asking, and the Google Keyword Planner will tell you how many searches a month that Google is registering for that question or topic. The higher the amount of searches there are for the questions you put into the Keyword Planner, the more your product will be in demand.

47.) More Places to Get Product Ideas

Here is a list of a few other places to look for Product ideas in your niche:

- ✓ **Google Trends** – Great for checking recent trends in your niche

- ✓ **Google AdWords**

- ✓ **Amazon** – Look through the amazon best-seller rankings to see how popular your niche really is. Type in your niche in the books section, sort the books by popularity and see how highly rated the top book in that niche is. Anything ranked under 50,000 is a hot niche!

- ✓ **Niche-Related Magazines** – Good for seeing what questions are being asked in your niche

- ✓ **Niche-Related Blogs** – Good for seeing niche-related conversation

- ✓ **Niche-Related Forums**

- ✓ **Clickbank**

- ✓ **Social Media** – Good for seeing niche conversation on groups and pages

- ✓ **Word of Mouth**

- ✓ **Yahoo! Answers** – See what questions people are asking

- ✓ **Quora** – A more sophisticated version of Yahoo! Answers.

Be sure to check out these and others to see what topics are hot in your niche!

48.) An Easy Product to Make for a Beginner…

Many beginners get tied up about what products to make, and where to start. If you do not have any expertise in your chosen niche, or just want to get started quickly, then here is an alternative method to the teleseminar method mentioned in tip number 45.

There are a huge array of experts in every niche, and these experts are always trying to get more exposure to potential clients.

Try this: make a list of 10 experts in your niche, ranging from the biggest players at 1-3 and the smallest at 7-10.

Contact number 10 first and ask for an interview – you will be surprised just how many of these experts will conduct interviews with you for free. They all want more exposure of course. If they do ask you to pay however, then it is worth paying up to £50 or so for a good interview, it will pay dividends later!

As you get more interviews done and get practiced, then you can begin to go up your list until you feel confident enough to approach number 1. Once you have all these interviews compiled, you can now batch them together into an interview series that you can sell, or give away as a freebie, or as a bonus product.

An interview series is an easy way to gain exposure in your niche and get a good product off the ground quickly. Besides, you will get your name in front of some of the big guns in your industry. If you forge good relationships with other business owners in your niche, then you can call on them to help you launch your products to their lists to increase your traffic and sales!

49.) The Difference Between a Free Giveaway and a Paid Product

There are several differences between a freebie and a paid product, but the most important is the goal you are looking to achieve for each. Let me explain...

When a customer comes to you with a problem, or when you make first contact with a customer through your marketing, they have a BIG, FAT HEADACHE! Yes, you read that correctly, they have a pain in their head that won't go away because it is caused by a problem that hasn't been dealt with - as they are missing the necessary information to deal with it.

With your freebies your main aim should be to *cure the customers' headache first*, so that they can see the benefit of listening to you and digesting your content. You may then redirect them into your mailing list, or sell them a product/service. This is where you will fix the *problem* that caused their headache in the first place!

We see many internet marketers who try and tackle the problem that the client has, before curing the pain that they are getting from it.

Let me ask you, if you had a headache, would you rather I give you a headache tablet to immediately cure your headache, or not do that and simply tell you how to avoid headaches in the future?

You would rather have the headache pill now, and listen to me later right?

This is the attitude of your customers... Make sure that you are solving their immediate pain first to gain trust (in your freebie), and then letting them know that you can fix the problem that caused that pain too, through your products and/or services.

Be sure that you have put some amazing painkiller content in your freebie, as customers will be more likely to buy your products if you do a fantastic job first time!

50.) 'Move the Free Line'

A great internet marketer, Eben Pagan, created a concept called 'Moving the Free Line', which basically means that the more you can give away for free in your business, then the higher the prices that you can command for your products.

The internet these days is based around free value, and if you are selling anything online, then you want to be giving away some of your best content for free to get people interested in buying your products.

When you are selling your products, be sure to pile on the value (in the form of freebies and bonuses), so that the perceived value of your product is higher – that way you can command a higher price. We call this *'stacking the offer'*, as you are continuously stacking more bonuses on the offer than the viewer could ever imagine, simply to be able to command a higher price.

Remember – never try to compete on price, compete on *value!*

51.) Put Your Valuable Content Behind a Membership Site

One great tip to prevent your paid content from being shared with others for free is to put your content onto a membership site where on purchase, the customer receives a set of login details and a password. They can then access the bought content by logging in online, instead of downloading it as a zip folder or similar.

This is mainly used for online courses, audio courses or video courses as they can easily be transferred and shared around, causing you to lose out on sales! But you can also put the download page for an eBook behind a membership site.

Another added bonus of holding your content on a membership site is that if you want to change any of the content at a later date, then you can do so with ease and without your customers having the out-dated version. For example, if you had a video course and had to re-shoot video 3 of your course, then you could simply take video 3 off the website and replace it with the new video at the click of a button.

This is an extremely easy way to keep your content up-to-date and relevant to your market.

52.) Give Yourself Deadlines to Meet

Don't let creating your products drag on and on… We see many internet marketers who have been working on their products for *years* and have never completed them, let alone sold them!

Make sure you give yourself deadlines for your product creation stage. These deadlines must revolve around how much time you actually have to put towards your internet business, but should be strict enough to keep you on-track and not let the process drag on.

When you have an internet business you have to motivate yourself, as you have nobody there nagging you to check that you have done everything! It can be very demoralizing when you don't make as much progress in your business as you would have hoped; and this is normally due to poor planning rather than a lack of effort.

Give yourself strict guidelines to meet to help keep yourself on track. These can be changed or extended if need be, but they will give you a valuable timeframe to work to. If it helps you, let somebody know what you are up to and get them to check up on your progress on a regular basis. This holds you accountable, and for many people, having somebody check on progress helps keep them motivated.

You can do it, we believe in you!

53.) Using Private Label Rights (PLR) Products

Private Label Rights products, or PLR products for short, are ready-made products that you can buy, edit and re-package or simply sell on as your own. They can be in any niche or on any topic, and anybody can buy them.

We personally feel that buying a PLR product and simply selling it on is very risky as a lot of PLR products are not of outstanding quality (that your clients will come to expect from you).

We don't generally use PLR products at all as we create all of our own content from scratch. But we would strongly advise those who are thinking about using them to go through them thoroughly and at least edit them before selling them.

The best thing to do if you are going to use PLR products is to split the content up (and edit it to better it), and then use that content in your own products, or blog posts. This means that any product that you eventually sell will have been written in your own voice. Your fans will love this, as it will have superior, high-quality content compared to the PLR content that you originally bought.

PLR content can be used, but use it wisely and with caution!

54.) Change the Format to Dramatically Change Your Results!

Changing the format of a product, or creating a similar product in multiple formats will enhance the results that you get from your business *dramatically.*

People will naturally gravitate towards products which suit their learning style. For example, visual learners may read eBooks, or look at videos, whereas those who learn best by hearing information may prefer listening to audios. Having different types of products in your business will allow you to cater for all needs.

Also, the value perception can also be changed by changing a product format, for example:

- A book may have a $20 value

- The same information in an online video course may have a $300-800 value

- The same information on flash cards may also sell for $20 (but at a bigger net profit to you).

Don't worry about a potential customer not wanting to buy a particular course of yours because it is similar to a book that you have written. People commonly buy the same content in a different format. This is likely because they want to take it in through a different medium. Some users also feel like they have accomplished something with they buy a new product, so they will keep buying them – even if they are very similar to something that they have bought before!

55.) Out-Sourcing Product Creation

If you are great at coming up with product plans, but hopeless when it comes to actually creating the product, then out-sourcing the product creation may be for you!

There are a few great places on the internet where you can go to hire people who can create your product/s for you. Two great places to start are Elance.com and Upwork.com. On these two sites, you can put up a job description of your product idea, and the rough scope of what you would like doing (but don't give them TOO much detail, save that until you have the right person to avoid somebody copying your idea). Professionals will then register their interest in taking on your job and you will be able to interview them and see their credentials, so that you can pick the right person.

I advise that you don't pick anybody new to do your job for you, and that you go for a mid-range price. Top price doesn't necessarily mean better work, and if you go for the bottom range then you may end up with a badly done job, as well as time and money wasted!

Another place to go are forums such as the Warrior Forum. There is a major section on the forum called 'Warriors For Hire' where you can advertise your interest in somebody creating products for you – and you may just find the diamond product creator that you are looking for!

56.) Always Give More Than They Bargained For!

THE biggest tip I can give you in relation to product creation is to <u>ALWAYS</u> over-deliver! Customers love to get MASSIVE VALUE and you should always make sure that you include plenty of juicy bonuses with your products - bonuses that your client might not have even known about until they log into your membership site or open up your eBook!

Clients will return to those who treat them well, and they will LOVE YOU if you pack your product full of additional freebies. Repeat business from your current and future customers will make you three, four – maybe even twenty times richer and more fulfilled!

Always be adding more value, always care for your customer and treat them like the friend they are to you. Always sort out any problems with your products and/or services promptly, and ALWAYS over-deliver to attract the clients, money and fulfilment that you love and deserve!

Chapter 4
Marketing and Sales

Marketing and sales are the life-blood of your company - and your profits. They reach out to your customers, new and old, and let them know what you have to offer and how you can help them. The products and systems are the bones of your business, and the marketing is the blood-flow which keeps it all moving and keeps it well fed with new clients and opportunities.

Most of marketing and sales is as much about the techniques that you use to market your products and services, and the means you reach your audience, as it is about what you actually say.

Many new internet marketers dabble in just about every marketing method possible to try and 'get rich quickly', instead of mastering a few forms of marketing before moving onto the next, to achieve solid results and a strong marketing foundation.

In this chapter, I want to remove the smoke and mirrors around the subject and give you plain, simple tips to achieve success in this crucial area of your business.

Enjoy!

57.) Paid Advertising vs. Free Advertising

All of your business's marketing can be split up into two categories: *paid advertising*, and *free advertising*.

Paid advertising generally involves adverts of some kind, these can be banner ads on forums, Facebook ads, Google Ads or a whole manner of different types.

Free advertising consists of more time-consuming tasks you can do to market your business for free, and to spread the word about your products and services. A few examples of free marketing are Social Media Marketing (excluding paid ads), Forum Marketing, Content Marketing, some JV releases etc.

The most obvious difference between these two types is the amount of money that you spend on each, but also free advertising generally takes up more time to implement, and the results may take longer to come through. With paid advertising you can market your products and sell them straight away, so you may not have to wait as long to sell as you would do with free marketing in some cases.

The real key to successful free marketing lies in tracking results, persistence and gaining momentum.

Paid advertising can also be scaled up massively once you have a marketing strategy that works well, and that suits your business model.

We would advise using a mixture of these two types of marketing. That mixture will depend on your budget and the time that you have available to put towards your internet business.

58.) Types of Marketing

As already mentioned marketing consists of free and paid marketing. Here are some examples of each type, this list is by no means exhaustive, but it provides most of the main players:

FREE –

- ✓ **Social Media Marketing** (Business Facebook, Business Twitter, LinkedIn, G+ etc.)

- ✓ **Forum Marketing** (being active on forums, with a link to your product, service or website in your signature file)

- ✓ **Some JV product launch or ad swaps** (if you do an ad swap and email each other's lists, or if a business partner launches your product to their list and you take a cut of the profit etc.)

- ✓ **Search Engine Optimization – SEO** (making your site search-engine friendly to attract traffic from search engines)

- ✓ **Networking** (networking with like-minded people, or people in your niche to spread the word and get referrals)

- ✓ **Educational Marketing** (giving away free information in the form of articles, videos or educational emails to educate viewers and get them to want more from you (to buy your products))

- ✓ **Guest Blogging** (blogging on a blog owned by somebody else to increase exposure, via a link back to your site or squeeze page)

- ✓ **Press Releases**

- ✓ **Video Marketing** (either by releasing videos on YouTube, or by using video marketing on your website etc.)

- ✓ **Article Marketing** (Publishing articles in a variety of forms that link back to your website for increased traffic)

PAID –

- ✓ **Google AdWords Adverts** (display adverts and search adverts)

- ✓ **Facebook Adverts**

- ✓ **LinkedIn Adverts**

- ✓ **Twitter Adverts**

- ✓ **Bing Ads** (and all other types of alternative paid website adverts)

- ✓ **Paid Banner Adverts** (on forums and websites)

- ✓ **Solo Ads** (Paying to advertise to someone else's email list)

- ✓ **WSO Product Releases** (Pay to release a product on the Warrior Forum – Internet Marketing niche)

- ✓ **Press Releases**

We recommend that you use a mixture of these advertising techniques to get your products and services marketed across a varied form of media, and to the largest potential audience.

59.) Hang Out Where Your Market Do

Ask yourself: where do my potential fans and clients hang out? The best way to get your message out there is to get into the thick of it, get into your customers head and think about the type of places they they look for information.

For example, if you were selling to corporate businesses, you wouldn't be marketing on Facebook or Twitter. You would be more likely to be doing LinkedIn ads, or Google Ads, as those are the sorts of places that corporate business owners hang out and look for answers to their problems.

Another great place to target the corporate market is by guest blogging on popular business blogs – this will gain you respect, authority and credibility.

Think about your niche market(s); imagine that you had their problems, fears, needs and desires, and think about where you would go to find answers if you were them!

Hone in and stay close to your niche market, and you will attract success with the right strategy.

60.) What is SEO? Is it Still Needed?

SEO stands for Search Engine Optimization and relates to making your site search engine friendly, so that you can attract more traffic from search engines. In the old days, back when the internet was new, you could create a site, 'SEO it', and have it display on the first page of Google in weeks. These days with much more web competition it is not so easy!

Google has an 'algorithm', which is basically a formula that they use to determine how far up the Google rankings your website comes. Google changes this algorithm frequently, and it can be a tricky job to keep up with it.

We will cover the two types of SEO in the next tip, but we advise that you do not focus *entirely* on SEO when you start. Many internet marketing experts admit to focusing too much on SEO when they first got started, which caused them to get little or no results! Until they changed their tact of course.

Some SEO is necessary on every website, but do use it alongside your other free and paid forms of marketing. If you solely rely on SEO these days then you will be left in the smoke by those marketers who simply pay for advertising and make money straight away. Remember, paid adverts come above the organic searches on Google anyway! Use a combined approach to be 100% effective in your marketing, and to create a well-balanced marketing plan.

61.) The Difference Between Local and Traditional SEO

Some internet marketers get confused between what local and traditional SEO entail, so we decided to clear up the topic for you so that you understand the difference, and know which relates to your business!

Traditional SEO is made up of several techniques that help your website get ranked higher by Google, these include:

- **Creating backlinks for your site** (creating links back to your site from other websites. These must be of good quality and not just spammed. Backlinks that are tracked will be 'dofollow' backlinks, and backlinks that won't be tracked are called 'nofollow' backlinks. Facebook and social media sites are 'nofollow', whereas quality posts on an article site with a guest article including your link would be a 'dofollow' link)

- **Filling out the on-page SEO** (this includes the meta-keywords, meta-description and meta-title for your blog articles which will tell the search engines that you have created new content, and what is included. It also includes having the keywords that you are trying to target – what you are writing about – in the title of your post)

- **Inter-linking your articles and pages** (to make it easier for the Google spider to index them all)

Local SEO on the other hand is all based around local companies. A company's local SEO is improved when Google has a lot of data relating to that company operating in one particular place, for example in a particular area in Chicago USA.

If you have a company that operates in one locality, then local SEO will be important for you, as with hard work, you will be able to come up on top in Google searches if customers in your area type in your service or product. This is simply because Google will create a link between your business and that particular area.

This can be done by including your location on your social media profiles and on your website, by getting your business on Google Local, by getting good reviews in your local area and by targeting Google Keywords which are to do with your local area (for example, 'butchers in Cambridge' for a butchers shop in Cambridge).

62.) Sell the Sizzle, Not the Sausage!

Have you ever come across the phrase **'sell the sizzle, not the sausage'**?

In a nutshell, the phrase simply means that you should not sell your products at face value to your customers; but instead you should sell what your product *can do for them*, what *problem it can solve*, and how it can *make their life so much better*!

Let's dig into this deeper... If you bought a new computer with an Intel i5 processor, you wouldn't buy it because you love the name of the processor or because you think the computer will look good on your desk as an ornament would you? You would buy that computer (with a powerful processor) simply because it is very quick (at the time of writing!), and because it is going to make your time searching online a whole lot *easier and quicker*.

In other words, you bought the computer with a fast processor because of what it can *do* for you, not because of what it is!

Apply this technique to your marketing, and sell the idea to the customer of what your product or service can *do for them,* how it will make them *feel* and how much *better* their life or business is going to be with your product. Apply this and you will see your sales rocket, as you are appealing to peoples' hearts - and not just their minds!

63.) Remember to F.O.C.U.S

F.O.C.U.S stands for Follow One Course of Action Until Successful!

The worst thing that a beginner internet marketer can do is to go out and try EVERY marketing approach on EVERY product type at the same time. Start simple - pick one product to start with, and pick one or two approaches to market that product. Focus on your desired outcome, and then go for it!

Of course, if the time comes that a particular approach is not working after repeatedly testing it, then tweak the plan to see if that changes anything. If it doesn't, then you may have to make a drastic change in your marketing or product plan, but be sure to not make any changes until you are totally certain that any one approach isn't going to work.

Remain streamlined in your intent, your goals and your plan and only focus on one thing at a time. All you need to know is the next step that you need to take anyway!

64.) Split-Test, Monitor and Improve!

When you are doing paid advertising using platforms such as Google AdWords, Facebook Adverts and the like, how you get those ads which convert at a HUGE rate is by split-testing and constantly improving your adverts. It is simply the only way to craft adverts that reliably results in a good stream of revenue for your business.

Split-testing involves creating a few different adverts in any of your advertising campaigns, and then comparing them to see which achieve the highest results.

Write 3-5 ads with different copy/images, and then split-test those to see which one gets the most results in say 50-100 clicks. You can then try and change the worst performing ads to try and beat the best performing adverts – so it becomes a constant process of bettering your ads until you are left with a series of highly-performing ads!

Don't fall in love with your ad copy, and make sure that you keep split-testing and improving to get more results in your business and to put your marketing budget to better use.

65.) Cross-Selling, Up-Selling & Down-Selling

To rapidly increase your business with minimal cost, you need to start using these **three** simple strategies, as they which will increase your sales exponentially:

Cross-selling involves selling a customer a related product or service to one that they just bought from you. For example, if an internet marketer had just sold an eBook on how to market for new business in a particular niche, then they could cross-sell that customer and give them a discount on a product they had just created on how to create products for that niche - so that their marketing knowledge can be put to use.

Up-selling involves asking a customer if they would like to upgrade what they have just bought, or get something bigger for not much cost. An example of this in an everyday business would be if you walked into a fast-food shop and bought a burger, and then were asked if you wanted fries for just another $1.50. This practice can be used in your internet business – for example, you could up-sell your customers to a full course instead of an eBook, for example.

Down-selling comes into play when a customer has said no to an offer of sale. For example, if you tried to sell a customer your new course on marketing for $1,000 on the phone, and they said no, you could then try and down-sell them to an eBook instead (which is much cheaper).

All of these techniques are extremely lucrative ways to expand your business, and we highly recommend that you use all three in your marketing funnels.

66.) Landing Pages – The Simple Way to Get Leads!

Landing pages go by many names - squeeze pages, opt-in pages and many more. Simply put, they all mean the same thing: an internet page that is marketed and where the viewer leaves their contact details (normally name and email address, or just their email address) in return for a free-giveaway that you are giving them in return.

Landing pages are pretty simple to set up, and there are several types of software that can be put onto your website to help you create them. We personally use OptimizePress, as it is extremely easy to use, and we can set up a landing page in minutes (check out our review of OptimizePress here - http://wp.me/p2twvK-6F). But there is also Kajabi, Leadpages and a couple of other programmes which do the same thing.

Some marketers opt to only capture the viewer's email when they give away the freebie, as it has a slightly higher opt-in rate... However in our experience, you get far better results from your email campaigns when you come to market to those leads if you have captured **both their name and their email**. This means you can use their name in your emails to them, which is obviously more personal. We want you to get the best results you can, so we highly recommend that you capture both their name **and** their email!

We wrote a blog article for you to show you the basics of setting up a squeeze page, you can check it here - http://wp.me/p2twvK-76.

67.) Thank-You Page Upsells

The thank-you page that you send your customers to when they sign up on one of your landing pages is **the last place that you will actually speak to all of those who have signed up to your list.** Some of those who sign up won't read your emails, but what is for sure is that they won't all read each and every one of your emails anyway!

Being the last place that everybody sees when they opt-into your email list, your thank-you page is the perfect place to upsell them to a product or service that you are offering with a discount.

For example, if somebody opted in to receive emails about internet marketing, you could upsell them to your $37 eBook (that you are selling for $17 especially for them on your thank-you page)!

This is a great technique to generate more sales, and as they have already said yes to your emails, there is more chance of them saying yes to buy your product/service at that moment... especially as you have reduced it especially for them!

68.) Social Media

Social media is a fantastic tool that you can use to engage with your niche market and to promote your online business activities; and what's even better is that it's free!

You can set up pages for your business on popular social media sites such as Facebook, Twitter, LinkedIn, Instagram and G+. These pages allow you to keep in contact with your customer base and 'mingle' in the thick of where your customers hang-out.

The most important thing to remember when using social media is to **add value**. You will get far more new customers from social media if you help them out first (for free), and then expect them to come back to you in the future and buy your products when they need answers.

Go onto related pages and groups on Facebook, answer peoples' questions and point them at free content on your blog. Let them know about freebies that you are giving away which could help them with their problem – never try to sell directly on social media unless you are doing a formal advert, which we will cover later on in this chapter.

Social media is an extremely powerful tool if used correctly. It does take a bit of time to get it going and create a following, but with time and effort, social media can supply your business with a steady stream of leads and customers.

69.) The Use of Educational Marketing

Educational marketing (also known as content marketing) is all based around giving away some of your content (for free) to showcase your work and add value to the customer. This will then entice them to buy your main products/services, as they will trust you and your content.

Educational marketing entails the use of your blog to give away free content in the form of articles, guest blogs on other sites, doing article syndication, or giving away free reports, books or courses. Educational marketing is basically any sales system whereby you give away free content to get the customer interested, with the aim to sell on the back-end.

Your blog is a great tool that you can use to write articles and give away lots of valuable information for *free.* And by the way, your blog is a VITAL part of your business, as it engages and keeps you in touch with your target market on a regular basis. Some internet marketers do not see the value in keeping up a free blog - they label it as a waste of time, stating that it doesn't directly make them money in their business.

For sure, it does take a bit of time and effort to write articles on a regular basis for your blog, but this can be outsourced if necessary.

Your blog will also indirectly make you a lot of money as it is a free resource that you can point your clients to in order to get them interested in what you have to offer. If your blog gets a lot of traffic, then you can also plant a few affiliate links in blog articles and get earning an income stream off the free content – cool right?

The fact is that if you don't have a blog, then your potential customers will put you behind every other business that does have a blog that gives (awesome) free content on a regular basis.

So make sure that you update your blog on a regular basis to keep those potential clients pouring in!

70.) Video Marketing – Powerful Stuff!

Video marketing is an extremely powerful form of marketing, as the viewer will most likely sees you in person on your videos. This means that the viewer can connect with you more readily, and will also trust you more, as you appear more personable on camera as opposed to in writing, or through other forms of online communication.

There are several types of videos that you can create to put out to your viewers. The main three types are: *Content videos*, *Sales Videos* and *Squeeze-Page Videos.*

Content videos are videos packed full of content for your viewer to learn from. This could be free content, or paid-for content, and these videos range from videos you put on YouTube, to professionally constructed videos to film content for an online course, or another paid product. The main point of content videos is to simply give informative content, and even though at the end of the video you may try and get the viewer to take an action, such as signing up to your email list, these videos are not normally salesy.

Sales videos are designed to get the viewer to take action and buy your products and/or services. They can sometimes provide a bit of content first to engage the viewer, and are for use on sales pages.

Squeeze Page videos are for use on squeeze pages where you want the viewer to opt-in to your email list in return for a freebie such as a free report or course. The main difference between these videos and sales videos is that you are giving away a freebie here and not selling a product, so it is easier to get the viewer to take action.

Use video marketing in your business to massively increase and educate your following, and to increase your conversions on squeeze and sales pages!

71.) Advert Stalking... Using Re-Marketing!

Have you ever heard that you have to contact a potential client 7-12 times before they will buy from you? This is mostly because your clients want to see that you are reputable, and a lot of your clients will need time to make the decision to buy, so the option should always be available to them.

Re-marketing is an extremely powerful way to get extra business by 'following' previous viewers of your adverts/content/products around the internet using what are called 'cookies' (cookies are files places on a viewer's website browser to track information), and then showing them ads to give them more chances to buy.

Let me explain...

Say for example somebody viewed a post on your blog that was all about how to sell using Google AdWords. You could enable a 'cookie' to be placed on that person's web browser (for a period of time, normally 30-60 days), which will automatically put them into a marketing campaign of yours for selling them a product to do with Google AdWords.

Clever right?

So using that marketing campaign, you can them set up adverts on Facebook, Google, Twitter, or on a whole manner of different advertising platforms to follow them around the internet and continuously promote your product.

Why this works so well is because as you *know* that they have registered an interest in Google AdWords (your product), and this makes them highly targeted and more likely to buy a product from you after consistent follow-ups.

Disclaimer: Please do be careful though, the laws around cookies are always changing, and you may need to have a cookie policy and reminder on your website.

72.) Forum Marketing – Get in Close to Your Customers

One fantastic place to do niche-related research, and also to market your products, is on online forums. Forums are great because you can get in close to your customers and have a personal conversation with them.

A great way to sell on forums is by using your signature file. Most forums allow you to have a 'signature' file which appears below your posts when you post on the forum. This is fully customizable, and you can use it to market what you have to offer people.

A word of warning – do not try and sell anything big in your signature file… The best approach is to give away a freebie to get people onto your email list, where they can be sold to from there. Always give first in anticipation to receive. Do check the forum rules for your niche-related forums as to whether you can include affiliate links as well as your own links, as different forums differ on this.

If you become a well-known member of a forum, then you will have more credibility, especially for doing forum marketing. Listen to questions people are asking and try and post genuinely useful information that will help those people in need. This is far better than writing lots of 'me too' type posts or irrelevant posts that will just get you banned. When you are well known, and you have a product that can genuinely help the potential client, then it will be far better received when you 'plug it' (direct somebody to a sale).

Forum marketing can take a bit of time to properly get going, but keep cracking at it and you will see results in the long-term. Just remember to give away freebies (or very low-cost products) in your signature file, and always provide relevant, useful information!

73.) Article Syndication

A really great way to raise the traffic to your website or squeeze page, that is totally free, is article syndication. Article syndication is the practice of submitting your articles - <u>after they are indexed on Google on your website/blog first</u> – to article sites such as EzineArticles.com with a call to action and a link back to your site at the end of the article.

Now why would you do that? The reason you would submit your articles is not so they can be found by readers, but by publishers who would want to use them on their own website. This means that if 10 people used your article on their website, then you would get 10 high-quality backlinks for your website from a website in a similar niche to yours. This will help your

Google rankings, but will also send streams of people back to your website, as your link will be embedded at the bottom of the article!

Now just a note, the fact that somebody else is publishing the same article as you is not harmful to your SEO, as if the article has been indexed on your website first, then there is no chance of their article ever appearing on a search engine. If you are still worried about it and don't want to take the risk, then it is a good idea to write separate articles to the ones that you publish on your website, and then embed your links into those and post them to EzineArticles.

Article syndication can take a little while to take effect, but in time it will get you hordes of targeted traffic to your website.

74.) Using Widgets to Sell on Your Website

Another way to sell on your website is by creating little adverts that run along the side of a webpage, these are a type of 'Widget' on a WordPress site.

Widgets are a great way to monetise a website when it has a following. They are especially great on the side of your blog as while viewers are flicking around your blog, the widget will catch their eye and then if clicked it can send them to a sales offer, opt-in form or anything else that you fancy!

I mentioned more about the actual mechanics of setting up a widget back in Chapter 1 (Creating a Website), please refer back there for more information on the setup process.

Use widgets to monetise your site, and increase your profits.

75.) Use Google AdWords to Generate Good Cash!

Google AdWords is THE biggest online advertising tool out there at the moment in terms of the reach that you can achieve.

The main difference between Google AdWords and many other advertising platforms is that the leads that come from Google AdWords are more qualified simply because they are actually *searching* for what you are offering! This is different to Facebook ads for example, where you just target a broad category of people who like a particular subject, and then they stumble upon your ad.

Google AdWords is all based around **Keywords** which are arranged into **Keyword Groups**. The Keywords, or phrases, are all based around what you think your market will be searching for on Google.

For example, if you were in the fishing niche, your market may be searching for phrases such as 'how to improve my fishing', or 'how to catch bigger fish'. The more targeted your Keywords are, the more targeted the audience that you reach will be.

Where the money is made in AdWords, is by only picking the Keywords which are *extremely* relevant to your business, or the products that you are selling. Too many businesses use too many irrelevant keywords and then wonder why they waste their advertising budget getting little results.

Stay niched, stay targeted, keep a clear sight on what you're selling and what the market demand is, and you will be fine.

76.) Using Facebook Adverts to Target Prospects While They are Relaxing!

Facebook ads are still fairly new (at the time of writing this book), and have only emerged in the past year or two onto the marketing circuit. Facebook marketing is totally different to Google AdWords marketing, simply because you are targeting your potential client while they are relaxing on Facebook, and not when they have specifically searched for your content.

There are two types of Facebook ads: ***newsfeed ads***, and ***side-bar ads***. These ads can be customized in all sorts of ways - for example there is an option to just target desktop computers, and you can change the copy, picture, video and the entire market that you are advertising to. We normally use more newsfeed ads, as they appear bigger on our potential client's homepage, and you can attract likes and comments on these ads which increases social proof for your marketing, branding and product.

We recommend that you do not try to sell anything too big on Facebook ads (anything over $50 dollars is too much, and even that is pushing it really!), as your customers are just milling around and are less likely to be in a buying mood. We normally aim to give away freebies such as free reports, or free webinars to get people involved in our business, rather than straight-sell to them straight away. Patience pays a big part here, and you need to develop a relationship with your prospects first.

You can create 'custom audiences' to create very targeted groups of individuals to market to by using a 'tracking pixel'. You can even insert these tracking pixels on a different website, so that you can market to them on Facebook! Check out the help section in Facebook to find out how to do this.

It is best to play around with Facebook ads with small amounts of funding, and split test them for best results.

On a side note, you can now put a link to a website of your choice at the end of videos that you post on

Facebook. This is a great way to direct prospects to your squeeze pages or sales pages, to get them into your marketing funnel.

77.) Solo Ads – Hijacking Others' Lists!

We use a lot of solo ads in our business; solo ads are **FANTASTIC** for getting a lot of fresh people to sign up to your email list, some of whom will eventually buy your products!

A solo ad is basically when you find somebody with a big email list in your niche, and then you pay them to be able to write an email to their list. That email normally contains the link to one of your squeeze pages where you offer a freebie in return for them signing up to your list – hence 'hijacking' another's list!

A common concern with Solo ads is what is known as 'click fraud'. Click fraud is when a solo ad provider basically gets everybody on his/her list to click on the links in the email that you send, but then not opt-in. This makes it look like your email has had lots of clicks, but you haven't actually got any sign-ups!

Normally, the only way to find a reputable solo ad provider is to work through word of mouth, and see who has had good experiences with a provider. However, recently we have found a great website for solo ads which has solved all of our problems with finding good providers!

The website is called Udimi, here is the link for you to check it out:

https://udimi.com/a/9m4w6

Udimi takes away all normal problems with Solo ads, and we have also found it very cost-effective.

Udimi has built-in software which automatically detects 'click bots' which are commonly used for click fraud. This takes away the prospect of becoming a victim of it, and to add to that, Udimi also have a rating system on the website, so that you can see how others have rated a particular vendor's service. This enables you to pick out the vendors who you would like to use who are tried and tested.

Udimi also has a great search feature, so you can search for the date that you would like to send out an email, the number of clicks that you would like, what niche you want to target and many other options. The programme will then automatically recommend the right vendors for you.

78.) If You Would Like to Sell Physical Products...

If you want to sell physical products in your online business, then there are several options available to you. Here are a few of our top tips...

For whatever physical product that you want to create, the physical components of that product are normally available online. For example if you are thinking about creating a physical DVD course, DVD boxes and plain DVDs (good quality) can be bought online, and then printed on using a good quality printer.

Always look to get the main components of your products online before looking for a marketing company to make them for you. It will take more time, buy it will save you a lot of money.

There are also fulfilment companies who provide a service where they hold your stock for you, and then send it out to your clients on an order-by-order basis. They normally charge a small fee per item, and this will save you holding stock at home - which normally takes up lots of room!

Amazon.com is also a fantastic resource for selling products online as they have a fulfilment arm and can dispatch stock for you; although their fees may be higher than normal fulfilment companies if they host your products online too.

Be clever in your research, and you will be able to produce physical products for less, and ship them out for peanuts!

79.) Get a Plan and Stick to it!

The most important thing to remember with your marketing is that you need to form a marketing plan **and then stick to it.** Too many beginner internet marketers try to do every marketing method in the book, only to end up over-whelmed and confused!

Too much knowledge can be a dangerous thing all at once, so pick 2-3 marketing methods you would like to try first, and then get cracking. If the results from your marketing are not what you expected after a while, then tweak parts of your plan until you get a marketing plan that works for you. Only change it if it doesn't work after testing!

Chapter 5
Affiliate Marketing

Affiliate marketing is the main strategy for making money online that most beginners investigate if they do not already have their own products to sell.

There can be a lot of confusion with affiliate marketing as many beginners try any and every technique to market affiliate offers that they can. This normally just results in *'me too' type marketing*, where they just leave the affiliate link on multiple websites without pre-selling at all.

And of course, that doesn't make many sales!

In this chapter we are going to cover the main strategies, tips and tricks to use when marketing affiliate offers, and give you a firm basis for going ahead and making money online by marketing affiliate offers.

Let's jump in!

80.) How Do I Find a Great Niche Market?

Let's start with the basics - how to find a niche to promote affiliate products in.

Now, where you start depends on your resources, if you already have a list or a business in a certain niche, then you are most likely going to want to start there - as you already have assets to help with your affiliate marketing.

However for those of you who don't have an email list of subscribers or a previous business, the best place to start is by researching online.

Think about your passions, what type of niche would you find it fun to sell in? Job satisfaction is a big factor in internet marketing, as you are going to spend a lot of time working in the niche that you choose!

After you have identified a market, such as the fitness market or internet marketing, jump on the Google Keyword planner and see how many people are searching for products in that market, and see what specific questions most of those people are typing into Google (identify your niche).

This is exactly the same process to find your niche market as in chapter one.

Once you know what people are asking for in your chosen niche, then it is much easier to go onto an affiliate site such as Clickbank or JVZoo and pick products to sell to that market, as you know exactly what they want!

I have also written a post on my blog about this subject which you may find helpful, check it out here - http://wp.me/p2twvK-94.

81.) Where Do I Find Affiliate Products to Promote?

There are two ways to find affiliate products to promote: you can use portal sites such as Clickbank.com or JVZoo.com to find products to promote, or you can go to individual companies who offer affiliate opportunities.

Sites such as Clickbank.com or JVZoo.com are a good place to start as they have hundreds of affiliate products which you can sell, all in one place. You can compare the products to see which are selling well at the moment, and browse to see which you would like to promote from a list of different niched products, eg. in Health and Fitness or Internet Marketing. We will cover how to find a good affiliate product to sell on these sites further on in the chapter.

There are also many independent sites and retailers of products and services that have information on their websites about their various affiliate programmes. For example, many websites such as those offering hosting, domain names and online products have affiliate services which you can sell through, and sales are tracked by using an affiliate tracking link.

82.) How Your Sales Can Be Tracked Online

Affiliate sales are normally tracked through a link called an *'affiliate link'*. This link will be individual to you, and if anybody visits a webpage through your link and buys a product or service, then the sale can be tracked and credited to you.

Most affiliate links also install something called a *'cookie'* on the visitor's web-browser for a certain period of time (this varies between providers, but is usually between 30-60 days). This means that if they re-visit the website at a later date and buy a product, then the sale is still credited to you – even if they did not specifically go through your link on the second time around.

Most affiliate providers offer a service where you can track how many views you've had through all your affiliate links, so that you can see how many sales each one has produced. This will help you keep track of your marketing campaigns so that you can keep a firm handle on your marketing spending vs. your results.

83.) 'Cloaking' Affiliate Links

For an affiliate, it is sometimes useful to be able to *'cloak'* your affiliate links - although do check with whoever you are being an affiliate for to check that they will allow you to do this.

To cloak your affiliate link basically means that those who you advertise to do not see your affiliate link, they will see either a shortened version, or a different link altogether. However, the cloaked link still takes them to the same page (through your affiliate link), and will still register as your sale if they buy anything.

Affiliate links can be cloaked at **both ends**, when the visitor first sees your link, and when they have actually landed on the page.

There are several WordPress plugins which will cloak your affiliate links for you – prettylinks and link cloaking by Cleon Pid are two which will allow you to simply put in your affiliate link and cloak them behind your domain name. For example you could turn:

"www.yourproduct1.com/wp2938hr8hfnf3r"

into

"www.theinternetmarketingplace.com/free-ebook", or something similar!

You always have to cloak an affiliate link behind a domain name that you own and it will appear as

"www.yourdomainname.com/yourchosenextension".

You can also cloak affiliate links in your hosting account, simply go onto 'link cloaking' and fill in the details to cloak your link.

84.) Split-Testing using Affiliate Links

Many affiliate sites will let you create multiple affiliate links so that you can split-test your marketing, and see which areas of your marketing are producing the most results.

For example, if you were marketing using 3 Facebook adverts and 3 Google adverts, you could create one set of links ending in **/facebook1**, **/facebook2** and **/facebook3**. You could then do the same for the Google adverts and create links ending in **/google1**, **/google2** and **/google3**.

This way when you sell a product, you can then accurately *track exactly which advert produced the sale,* and over time, you can see exactly which areas of your marketing are producing the most sales.

Keep split-testing and aim to cut back on the marketing that is not working - so that you can increase the marketing which is working, to produce the greatest results.

85.) Picking the Right Affiliate Product to Promote

Picking the right affiliate product to promote can be the difference between success and failure as an affiliate marketer!

A fantastic business consists of a fantastic product/service and fantastic customer service, and seeing as the owner of the product will be providing the customer service, you should be entirely focused on finding a great product to promote.

There are a few things to take into account when looking for the right product, here they are:

- **Is there actual demand in the market for the product(s) that you are thinking about promoting?** You can test this by looking at the previous sales results of the product, and by researching on forums and on the Google Keyword Planner to see if people are searching for the answers/solutions that the product provides.

- **Does the product have a great sales page and a great customer experience?** As you cannot control what happens after you drive the traffic to the offer, you need to make sure that the sales page and the follow-up content is sufficient enough to convert the traffic that you bring into paying customers.

- **Are there any resources available for you as an affiliate?** Resources can be extremely helpful when driving traffic to the product offer, and can make your job a lot easier as an affiliate. Resources can commonly include made-for-you banners for banner ads, and email and advert text that is ready for use.

- **Do you actually believe in the product?** Have you had an experience of it? I *highly* recommend that you only sell products that you fully believe in. Never sell anything just to make a quick-buck. Your name and reputation is invaluable, and you don't want it to be tarnished in the industry because you tried to make a quick bit of money!

Be sure to take time deciding which product(s) that you would like to promote; it is an extremely important decision to get right.

86.) Don't Be a 'Me Too' Type of Affiliate!

A lot of new affiliate marketers try and present their affiliate offers in a *'me too'* sort of way by simply posting their affiliate links all over the internet, without pre-selling the product at all.

To be an effective affiliate, and to make good commissions, you need to be presenting the products in the best way possible in order to engage the customer and get them interested in learning more.

Depending on the type of products that you are looking to be an affiliate for, you should consider setting up your own website page for the product. On here you can give your opinions of the product and why it is such a good product to buy (a personal testimonial). You can also include other testimonials which you have gathered for it, or even those from the sales website.

Creating a video and posting it to **YouTube.com** can also be a great way to review affiliate products, as YouTube videos can rank highly in Google searches quite easily with a little bit of effort (and some backlinks!).

With a lot of products that you can find to promote on sites such as clickbank.com, the sales pages for the products could be greatly improved. As you can't do this yourself, it is wise to create your own page to 'pre-sell' to your potential customers.

87.) Affiliate Marketing as a Business, or a Second Income Stream?

Affiliate marketing is fantastic! You get paid well to sell somebody else's product that you didn't have to spend the time to create. Affiliate marketing is one of the most common ways that beginners get into internet marketing, but what would you like **YOUR** path to be?

You see, affiliate marketing is great, but I strongly suggest that you think about whether you want affiliate marketing to be the main core of your business.

There are a few potential downsides to affiliate marketing to be aware of:

- When you market somebody else's product you **do not control the sales funnel**. You could lose a lot of money marketing an affiliate offer that doesn't convert well (this is why choosing the right offer is **so** important!).

- You don't own the products, so you could build a whole business on the back of an affiliate product only for the product to simply be removed from the market – leaving you with no business left.

- It can be a lot harder to build an email list when marketing somebody else's product.

Now I am not saying that affiliate marketing is a bad idea – in fact far from it! But I would urge you to consider whether you would like to solely be an affiliate marketer, or whether you would like your own products in the future.

In internet marketing, we have to think about sustainability as well as profit, and taking the correct measures early on ensures that your business is built on a foundation of rock and not sand; as a foundation of rock won't wash away suddenly.

88.) Give Away Your Freebie Too!

One way in which you can be different from the other affiliates marketing the same products as you is by **giving away your freebie along-side the paid product** if you have your own sales page. This is also a great way to capture the details of the lead as they will have to enter their details for you to email your freebie to them (like on a squeeze page).

Giving away your own freebie in addition to the sale of the affiliate product not only gives additional value for the customer buying the affiliate product, but it also gives them the opportunity to sample your products/services. This could potentially end up in a sale of your own paid products down the line as well if they like your content.

It pays to be different, keep building the value for your customers and they will never buy from anybody else!

89.) Only Sell What You Believe in

We as professionals in our business only promote affiliate products which we believe in, and which we know will genuinely help those who will be buying them.

As a rule: **NEVER** be an affiliate for a product unless you are convinced that it will genuinely help those who are buying it. You would think that this goes without saying, but you would be surprised how many new internet marketers on the scene promote products that they have not spent any time testing, or at least looked into to check that they are legitimate – all in order to just make a quick buck online!

There is too much to lose by promoting a product that is awful, and wasting peoples' time and money – you have your reputation at stake.

We normally buy the products which we market so we can check them, and so we know that what we are selling is legitimate. You do not have to do this, but at least do some background research on the internet to check that what the product claims to do can actually work, and that it seems legitimate.

Rant over, but better safe than sorry!

90.) Setting up Your Own Affiliate System – The Kit

Setting up a system to affiliate your products will be a HUGE boost to your business, simply because others will be able to sell your products for you – and you will be able to earn passive income from that.

There are many systems that you can use to affiliate your products, but the best one that we have come across BY FAR is Infusionsoft.

Infusionsoft really does do the job well when it comes to organizing affiliates. In a nutshell, you can add referral partners manually (or get them to sign up on a page), and once they are signed up, they can actually log-in to their own personal end of your Infusionsoft. This allows them to see what commissions they have earned, and what percentage they will get for selling certain products - saving you from having to constantly update your affiliates manually as to what they have earned.

Infusionsoft is both a CRM system, an Auto-Responder, and it has an affiliate centre too, so you can have all of your contacts in the same place. This saves the hassle of having to get several bits of software to talk to one another.

You can check out Infusionsoft on your *Resources Page*.

91.) Setting up Your Own Affiliate System – The Affiliate Offer

The most important part of setting up your affiliate system is actually deciding how much you will pay your affiliates, and what business plan you want to use.

The simplest way of working with affiliates is to give them a flat-rate cut of each product that they sell. This normally ranges from 50% to as high as 95% in some cases.

The other way to work with affiliates is to split your products into two sections, up-front products, and back-end products. The total commission from the up-front products can then be given to the affiliate. You then make your money on the back-end (and may also give them a split of the back-end too).

This second strategy may seem crazy at first – why would you give *ALL* the hard-earned commissions from the up-front products that *you* spent time creating to your affiliates?

Well, this strategy is becoming more popular with those who have affiliates, and it is used simply to win over affiliates and to get them to affiliate for you, and not somebody else.

Let's face it – there are lots of affiliate opportunities out there which are paying very high commissions. You need to be **different**!

So to round up, you need to choose your strategy: have a normal commission split with your affiliates, or give them 100% of the front-end products, so that you make your money on the back-end products.

92.) The Real Trick to Promoting Affiliate Products...

Many new affiliates think that they can just open up an account with Clickbank or another similar affiliate site, grab a few affiliate links, drop them in a few places on the internet and make money.

You see, in **any** type of sales, whether online or offline, the key is to establish **trust**. And to establish trust, you must be in frequent contact with those who you are selling to.

So here is the real key: build an email list of subscribers, give them some GREAT content, and then promote affiliate offers to them once in a while. The standard rule is to send at least three emails with good, free content (emailing every few days), and then email them with one sales email. This process can then be repeated!

You can mix things up by having discounts and bargain days, but remember that the key is **building up that trust with your prospects** before you ask for the sale. You always need to be establishing rapport, because people only buy from others that they like and trust!

93.) YouTube Reviews

A great way to market an affiliate product is by giving a review; a video review is exceptionally powerful because as the viewer can hear (and sometimes see) an actual person speaking - so trust can be easily built.

We have established that people only buy from those that they like and trust. If you give an honest review on YouTube of an affiliate product that you have tried yourself, then others will automatically trust you more, and will be more likely to buy the same product through your affiliate link.

YouTube reviews can also easily be embedded into your blog to act as an informative review, along with your affiliate link. So you may also get comments from your readers thanking you for the useful recommendation – success!

Make sure that you type in the product name that you are promoting at the start of your video title, and include it in the description and the tags. This is on-video SEO, and it helps rank your video highly in Google ranking (for reviews of that product) so that you can get organic traffic landing on your video - which will turn into sales.

Getting backlinks to these videos will also help them rank highly on Google. A backlink is simply a link on your website, or somebody else's website that links to your YouTube video. Build up backlinks to increase the number of views on your videos!

94.) Using Facebook Adverts

We covered the basics of Facebook ads back in Chapter 3, but it is poignant to say that Facebook ads are a fantastic tool to use in your affiliate marketing.

It is best to use Facebook ads to get those in your niche market to sign up to your email list - by offering them a freebie. To do this you will need to create a squeeze page for your freebie (a page where you offer the freebie to others in return for them filling in their contact details).

After you have created your squeeze page, you can easily set up a targeted Facebook advert to direct people to your squeeze page.

Once they have opted into your list, be sure to send them a few emails with some great content so that they learn to trust you, and like the information that you bring them. You can them periodically send them affiliate offers, and as they feel like they know and trust you, the response will be much greater!

95.) Using Facebook Re-Targeting to Get Additional Sales

Facebook's re-targeting system will get you lots of sales that you otherwise would have lost.

Have you ever heard that when selling, you have to present somebody with an offer up to *12 times* before they will buy?

Well that is also true in Internet Marketing sometimes!

The beauty of using re-targeting for affiliate products is shown when mixed with email marketing. When you come to send out a bulk email to your list, if you send them to a page where you pre-sell the affiliate product before you direct them to the sales website, then you can put a Facebook tracking code on the website page that will automatically add each viewer of that page to a Facebook *'custom audience'* if they do not buy.

You can then set up targeted ads in Facebook, aimed at that custom audience who didn't buy, which will follow them around Facebook and market to them. These ads will be promoting your affiliate product (that they didn't end up buying) – and naturally some of those who didn't buy your affiliate product the first time will now end up buying.

You see, when your prospects first look at your sales page they might be out with the kids, or on the phone – commonly causing them to end up forgetting about it.

Re-targeting allows you to remind these people of your offer on a constant basis until they buy.

We also covered re-targeting in Chapter 3, please refer back there for more information on re-targeting!

96.) Use Google AdSense for an Extra Income

Google AdSense is another way that you can monetise a blog that has a decent following. What Google AdSense does is display related adverts from Google down the side of your website (you can make these relevant to your fan base), so that you can earn money each time an ad is clicked and somebody buys.

Google AdSense is free to start using, but earnings differ depending on which products you sell, and in which niche you operate in. It is advisable that you put AdSense on your website when you have a decent fan base if you are thinking of doing so - otherwise you may not see many results if you do not have enough traffic!

You can sign up for Google AdSense below: http://tinyurl.com/mw3u3jt.

We don't currently use Google AdSense as a source of revenue, but it is another tool in the toolbox for your website if you choose to use it!

97.) Supply vs. Demand

There is one more phenomenon to be aware of in affiliate marketing, and when marketing products in general, and that is the law of supply and demand.

You see, the price/demand of a product goes up when it is in short supply, just as the price/demand of a product generally goes down when there is a large supply.

Therefore, it is important that you pick a product to market as an affiliate that is not already flooded in the market, so that it is not already being marketed by many others – as the whole market may already have heard of it. If the market is flooded with a product then the demand for that product will reduce, dropping your sales potential.

Make sure that your chosen affiliate product is something that the market will want, and potentially something that the market is short of, to give your marketing the best chance of success!

Chapter 6

A Few Last Pointers…

Congratulations! As you have got this far, I have no doubt in my mind that you are committed enough to your dreams to become a truly fantastic internet marketer – I believe in you.

Now for the last few tips, I would like to give you a few general success habits that are used by the top internet marketers, and that will prove useful in your business journey.

Read them, take them in and use them, and I have every faith that if you work hard, then your dreams will become a reality.

98.) Always Be Bettering Your Business

In other words, play the long game.

Building a business is a journey, it won't happen overnight.

'It takes a lot of work to become an overnight success.'

Work on your business every day, taking small steps towards your goals, and you will get there in the end. Don't be annoyed with yourself if you make a mistake when you are starting – we all make mistakes I can guarantee you that! Just take baby steps towards your goal and it will become a reality.

Persistence is the name of the game here. If it was easy, everybody would do it!

99.) Be Your Own (Brilliant) Boss!

One note about working for yourself – most likely at home.

You are *your own boss*! That means that there isn't somebody annoying there to nag you about finishing off all your daily tasks, or to get a project or product done on time – it is all up to **you**!

Now, even though it can be a great feeling to ditch the job (and the external boss), it does come with drawbacks. You will have to motivate yourself more than ever, and it will be up to you to make sure that everything gets done, and that you are working to your full potential.

So enjoy the freedoms of working from home - such as being able to have as many cups of tea as you want during the day, or being able to start and stop work when you like; but do make sure that you keep a firm handle on yourself and your business.

I believe that the key to being productive when working from home is to keep a strict regime, and to try to form good habits that will keep you on track. This could be waking up at the same time every day, or planning out your day into time slots. Whatever floats your boat!

Remain productive to get great results.

100.) Always Consistently Invest in Yourself

Always develop your greatest asset – **you!**

Your own knowledge is critical to your success, so keep learning and re-investing in your knowledge to expand your business exponentially.

Besides, even when great entrepreneurs such as Donald Trump lost all their money and hit rock bottom, what get them back out? *Their knowledge!*

Your knowledge is the one thing that can't be taken away, even if you lose your business. Think of it as a permanent investment.

So keep re-investing in yourself and create what I like to think of as a growing whirlwind effect. The more you invest in knowledge and **apply** what you have learnt, the more profit you make, and the more you invest next time to make more profit next time, and so on.

101.) Remember to Have Fun!

Running an internet business, or any business for that matter, is hard work. There's no doubt about that. But the most important thing you can do in your business is to remember to have **fun!**

You got into your business to build wealth and to be happy and free right?

So why not start now?

Remember to take regular breaks throughout the day and still get outside. Many internet entrepreneurs spend so much time on the computer that it is easy to start to slack on your health.

And if you don't have your health then you have nothing.

Treat yourself well, have fun and allow yourself to relax at the end of the day when you have done all that you can. Mastering your work/life balance over a period of time is the key to having an awesome business, and a fantastic lifestyle!

The Next Steps...

Are up to you.

You can have all the knowledge in the world, but do you know what really pays?

Consistent action towards your dreams.

If you are excited by the idea of turning your dreams into a reality and having a sustainable internet business that lets you live the life of your dreams, then take what I have taught you in this book, and **put it into action.**

Get the ball rolling – getting started is always the hardest thing.

And if times get hard, keep believing, and keep pushing on... Because you could be just one push from success!

Make sure to keep re-investing in yourself and your education, because intellectual property really does pay dividends in the long-run; and your knowledge is the major factor that separates you from the average man or woman on the street.

Oh, and once you have reached your goals, remember to give back to those who supported you on the way up, and those in need of your help. It really is rewarding.

"The true measure of a man is how he treats someone who can do him absolutely no good." – Ann Landers

About The Author

Having been born into an Entrepreneurial family in Gloucester UK, Christian was always destined to be an Entrepreneur. From a young age he got involved in several business activities including internet marketing, and trading (gold) through a family contact.

Upon leaving formal education at 18, Christian decided to avoid University, to go down his own path of discovery into business. Having initially gone into packaging and selling property investment deals as a business, he soon realised that it was not his passion, and that it was far more beneficial to use property investment simply as an investment strategy – and to build a business in another area.

After brainstorming, going back-and-forth, and changing plans, Christian finally decided to go back to his roots and start up an internet marketing business with his business and life partner, Joanne Moore.

To get started, they began to help corporate clients; they decided to put their skills to use by helping a company in the property industry market their services to their clients on an upcoming sales launch that they were doing. Christian and Joanne were able to make a big impact - delivering them 105 sales in 3 days. Here's what Rob Moore (Co-Founder of Progressive Property) had to say:

"Christian and Joanne helped us market our most recent product for lead generation using a P&P offer that we had never promoted before. The results they delivered were fantastic, delivering 105 sales in a 3 day launch period. We had never used a paid product during a launch strategy before, but it is definitely a strategy that was helped by their marketing prowess and we're looking forward to working with them again during our next launch – Thanks guys!" - Rob Moore, Co-Founder of Progressive Property, £25 Million JV Partner.

After the success achieved during that launch, Christian and Joanne began to attract more and more clients - all of whom wanted them to help market their company online to create more sales, and higher profits.

"If you want to leverage time, costs and technology (internet marketing and its related functions) you should speak to Christian. You will not be disappointed!" – Adrian Walker, Director of Amassing Greater Wealth LTD.

After successfully helping a few clients increase their presence online (in both large and small businesses), Christian and Joanne came to the realisation that anybody could do what they did...

Anybody could set up an internet marketing business in an area that they are passionate about - from an idea, or from a particular area of knowledge, which could set them free from an everyday job, and increase their quality of life.

And that is why Christian and Joanne set up **The Internet Marketing Place**: because they are passionate about helping individuals reach financial freedom online, by building a profitable internet business that they **love**.

There is so much potential online, and the number of web visitors is increasing year-on-year; making the opportunities online more and more exciting.

Christian's mission for this book is to reach out aspiring internet marketers - to give them solid tips and information that they can go away and implement into their internet business to increase, profit, freedom and happiness.

Website - www.TheInternetMarketingPlace.com

Chat with us on Facebook! –
https://www.facebook.com/theinternetmarketingplace

Send us a Tweet @InterMarkPlace! –
https://twitter.com/InterMarkPlace

Catch up with us on G+! -
https://plus.google.com/+TheinternetmarketingplaceGPlus/

I have also included a free resources page with this book, please visit the link below to access it!

Visit This Link for Your Free Internet Resources Page - http://wp.me/P2twvK-b4

Also, be sure to go to the link below to grab your **free copy of our eBook** 'The 7 Horrendous Mistakes Beginner Internet Marketers Make in Their Business That Stop Them From Ever Making Any Money Online!"

Here's The Link to Claim Your Free eBook - http://wp.me/P2twvK-n6

One Last Thing…

As you purchased this book, Amazon will give you the chance to rate it online, and to leave a review if you wish.

If you enjoyed reading this book, and if you think that your friends/business associates would benefit from giving it a read, then please would you take a few seconds to give them a heads up about it?

After all, if it turns out to make a big difference in their lives and/or business, then they will be forever grateful to you – as will I. And the next round of drinks will be on them!

I also value and appreciate all feedback online in the form of ratings and reviews; it warms my heart to know that my books are helping others, and the constant process of feedback helps me improve my work to add even more value in the future.

Thank you for taking the time to read my work, and thank you for making my dream of helping others become a reality.

To Your Continued Success!

Christian.

Notes:

Notes:

Notes:

© Christian Swift - 2014 & Onwards.

www.ingramcontent.com/pod-product-compliance
Lightning Source LLC
Chambersburg PA
CBHW072047190526
45165CB00019B/2065